THE NAVAJO PEACE TREATY
1868

Woman weaving outside her hogan on the Navajo Reservation, Arizona-New Mexico. Photographer and date not recorded; possibly E. H. Maude, 1890s. Courtesy Smithsonian Institution National Anthropological Archives, Bureau of American Ethnology Collection.

THE NAVAJO PEACE TREATY 1868

by

MARIE MITCHELL

FIRST EDITION

Mason & Lipscomb

PUBLISHERS NEW YORK 1973

Copyright © Mason & Lipscomb Publishers, Inc. 1973

Published simultaneously in the United Kingdom by Mason & Lipscomb, London, England

Library of Congress Card Number: 73–6859

International Standard Book Number: 0–88405–022–X

First Printing

Printed in the United States of America

Library of Congress Cataloging in Publication Data

Mitchell, Marie.
    The Navajo peace treaty—1868.

    (Great events in world history)
    Bibliography: p.
    1. Navajo Indians—Government relations.
2. Navajo Indians—History. I. Title.
E99.N3M65   970.5   73–6859
ISBN 0–88405–022–X

Contents

	LIST OF ILLUSTRATIONS	vii
	PREFACE	ix
	ACKNOWLEDGMENTS	xi
1	*The First Americans Were Indians*	1
2	*The Invaders*	9
3	*The Mexican Revolution*	17
4	*The Army of the West*	24
5	*Fort Defiance*	33
6	*Tensions Mount*	44
7	*The Civil War Period*	51
8	*Destroy and Conquer*	62
9	*Invasion of Canyon de Chelly*	69
10	*The Bosque Redondo*	78
11	*The Treaty of Peace*	90
12	*A New Beginning*	99
13	*Gradual Progress*	107
14	*The Railroad*	117
15	*Dogged Perseverance*	124
16	*Years of Fulfillment*	133
	NOTES	139
	BIBLIOGRAPHY	143
	INDEX	

List of Illustrations

Woman weaving outside her hogan on the Navajo
Reservation, Arizona-New Mexico   frontispiece

Map of Navajo Country   4–5

The Old Santa Fe Trail. From Henry Inman, *The Old
Santa Fe Trail* (1897)   20

The Canyon de Chelly   34

Fort Defiance at Canyon Bonito, New Mexico
From an engraving of a drawing by Lt. Col.
J. H. Eaton, USA   38

Fort Defiance, Indian Agency,
Arizona, today   39

General William T. Sherman   47

Barboncito, Navajo chief, photographed
before 1870   53

Manuelito, noted Navajo war chief of
1855–1872, was photographed while
visiting Washington, D.C. in 1874   60

Colonel Christopher (Kit) Carson,
photographed in the early 1860s   65

Fort Sumner, New Mexico. Old post on
the Pecos River   80

Newspaper article about the Navajo Peace
Treaty from *The New Mexican*, June 9, 1868   92

Group of Navajo with Governor W. F. B. Arny,
Navajo agent at Fort Defiance,
Arizona, 1874–1875   94

Handwritten article of the Navajo Peace Treaty
and signatures of General Sherman and another
peace commissioner and of Navajo chiefs on the
treaty document   96–97

Another great natural resource of the Navajo—
the skill of their people. A Navajo grandmother
prepares her yarn for weaving   128

officers, was then authorized to investigate the situation and report the findings.

The Treaty of Peace was signed June 1, 1868, by ten officers of the United States Army and 29 Navajo headmen. Since that eventful day, the Navajo have lived through many drastic changes, but they have persevered. Today they are not only the largest Indian tribe in the United States, but also the richest and the most progressive.

Only the highlights of their progress can be touched upon here. It is hoped that this book will help the reader to understand better these early Americans and respect them for what they were and now are—and to ignore what we have sometimes been led to believe.

Preface

THE NAVAJO PEACE Treaty, negotiated between the United States government and the Navajo tribe of Indians, June 1, 1868, brought to an end one of the most tragic and dramatic periods in the history of this great nation.

Sometimes we Americans are prone to forget that this country is ours, not by right, but by conquest—that it took three centuries of brutal fighting, first by Spaniards, then by Mexicans, and then by Anglo-Americans, to achieve victory. But even then the courageous Navajo were not brought to terms until after the United States government commissioned the famous scout and Indian fighter, Colonel Christopher (Kit) Carson, to conquer them, no matter what the cost in lives or property.

During the spring of 1864, more than 7,000 Navajo men, women, and children were driven like cattle across the barren, mesquite-studded plains of New Mexico to Fort Sumner, where a reservation held them prisoners for four long years—four years of hardships, disease, and near starvation—before their plight reached the ears of the newly reorganized Peace Commission in Washington, D.C. General William T. Sherman, together with nine other

Acknowledgments

My sincere thanks are due to Peter MacDonald, Chairman, Navajo Tribal Council; to Daniel Peaches, Director of Navajo Public Affairs; and to Dr. Ned A. Hatathli, President, Navajo Community College, and his staff for sending me material I could use in this book, thereby making it all the more interesting to the reader.

My sincere thanks are owed to Dr. Martin Link, Curator, Navajo Tribal Museum, and to Robert Young, Tribal Operations Officer, Bureau of Indian Affairs, Albuquerque, for courtesies extended to me.

In addition, my sincere thanks are due to Gil Sweet, Regional Manager, Atchison, Topeka and Santa Fe Railroad; to H. A. Samson, Sgt., United States Marine Corps, 9th Marine District Headquarters; and to the many others who aided in my research for this book.

Marie Mitchell

1. The First Americans Were Indians

THERE IS NO proof of when the people we now call Indians first came to America. It is generally agreed that these prehistoric nomads migrated from Asia by way of the Bering Straits after the Ice Age, some 30,000 years ago. It is also agreed that they came in comparatively small groups over a long period of time. Even though they looked somewhat alike, they were of different tribes and spoke different languages.

Since there were no horses or mules in this country at that time, transportation for these early travelers was slow. The only domesticated animals they had brought with them were dogs.

Evidently, they had to carry their few possessions, which included fire in the form of live embers on a bed of clay in hollow gourds and some few crude tools and weapons, such as stone-tipped javelins, bone or stone scrapers, and daggers or darts for killing game for food. Such tools and weapons made it possible for them to survive as they spread out over this huge continent from Alaska to Peru, from the Pacific Ocean to the Atlantic.

They followed the trails of game animals. The flesh of such animals not only provided food, but the hides when

1

tanned, cut with stone knives, and sewed together by bone needles threaded with sinew, also provided them with warm clothing during the cold winter months. They probably wore very little clothing during the summers.

One of these migrating Indian bands has become known as the Navajo. Its early members settled in the sandy, rockbound region of the Southwest. The Diné they called themselves—meaning "The People."

The Navajo were, and still are, a distinctively different tribe of Indians. They do not accept the theory that they originate from some prehistoric tribe that wandered across the Bering Strait in the far distant past. Briefly, the Diné have maintained that they evolved through a series of worlds and stages of development in the evolution of life. According to this tradition, when the world was still young, it was a world of darkness—jet black. The second world or stage of development was a world of blue; the third, a world of yellow; and the fourth, a world of white, from which they emerged into the present world of primeval forests, high mountains, deep canyons, and fertile valleys.

This final world they believed to be bounded by four sacred mountains, mountains that had been created by the Holy Ones. To the east, these Holy Ones had created a mountain of white shell and named it Sisnajani (Mt. Blanca, San Luis Valley, Colorado). To the south, they had created a mountain of blue turquoise, Tso Dzil' (Mt. Taylor, north of Laguna, New Mexico); to the west, a mountain of yellow abalone, Dook'o'oslid (San Francisco Mountains, near Flagstaff, Arizona); and to the north, a mountain of jet black, Dibentsaa (Mt. Hesperus, La Plata Mountains, Colorado).

All the land within the confines of these four sacred mountains was given to the Navajo by their ancestors, First Man and First Woman. Here they lived for hundreds, perhaps thousands, of years in dignity and harmony with all the forms of plant and animal life. Here they sang their sacred prayer songs and conducted their religious ceremonies as the Holy Ones had taught them.

Four was a sacred number. There not only were four mountains, there were four colors; black, white, yellow, and blue. The Navajo were especially fond of the blue turquoise stones found in the vicinity of Tso Dzil' (Mt. Taylor) and considered them a gift of the gods.

Once when the sky was clear, so legend said, the Bearer of the Sun had ridden forth on a blue turquoise cloud, and some of the beautiful stones had fallen to the ground. These blue stones became the Navajos' most prized possessions and a part of most eceremonial rites just as were all the forces of nature—the earth, sun, wind, water, thunder, lightning, and rainbows—which symbolized supernatural powers and explained the Navajos' relationship to the earth and to plant and animal life.

Sickness, the Navajo believed, was an outward sign of evil. Their healing was mainly centered upon bringing the sick one back into harmony with the universe. The most powerful healing rites were sand paintings, which the medicine men began at sunrise and destroyed at sundown. "The gods were the first to draw sand paintings," the Diné were told. "The gods painted them on black clouds."

The Navajo did not have black clouds to paint on, but they did have colorful rocks and minerals for paint and the golden white sands of the desert as background. Only the medicine men, who had been trained from childhood for this purpose, could perform healing or other ceremonial rites. There also were chants and prayers for healing; for providing food; for blessing a baby, a hogan, or a wedding.

The hogans were dome-shaped structures made of

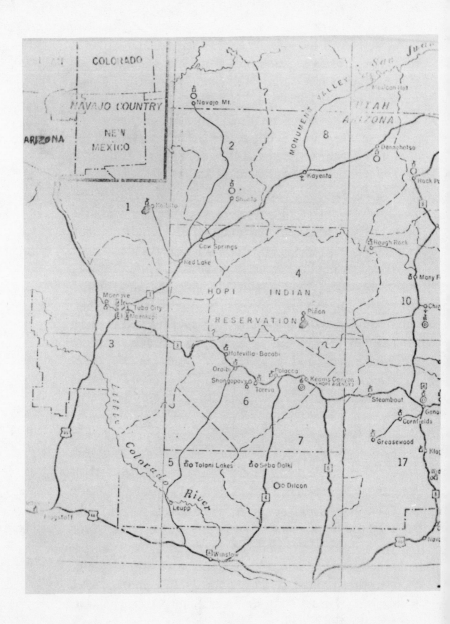

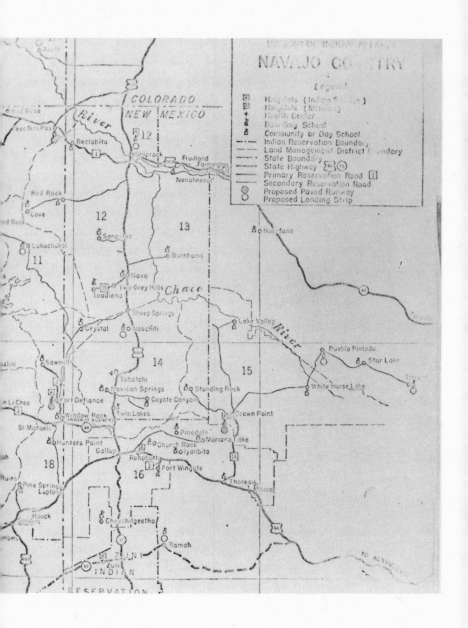

crossed poles covered with bark and plastered with mud. The openings faced the east, for according to tradition, the gods had made the first hogans so that they would always face the rays of the morning sun and the arching rays of the rainbow could span them from north to south. When finished, a hogan was blessed by the clan's own medicine man, who always carried sacred corn pollen and meal in a leather pouch for this and other purposes.

The colorful kernels of Indian corn also corresponded to the four colors of the four sacred mountains. Corn was a sacred food. Folk tales and legends have since been written of how the so-called savages first discovered corn; however, its antiquity was proved several years ago when corn pollen was found in samples of strata brought up from the bottom of a deep well in the vicinity of Mexico City. Moreover, corncobs have been found in excavations, which, when tested, date back to about 5,000 B.C.

Modern scientists, searching diligently for the true ancestry of this important food plant, have succeeded in finding some wild grasses related to this grain, but not the plant itself. Recently, the domestication of this native plant by the American Indians was acclaimed as one of the most important contributions to agricultural history, as corn is one of the most important cereal grains in the world. The other two are wheat from Africa and rice from Asia.

Corn, however, was not the only wild plant the prehistoric Indians discovered. They learned to spin the fibers of a plant we now call cotton and weave it on handmade looms into colorful rugs and blankets. Some historians believe the Navajo learned how to weave from the Pueblo Indians. But more recent research has disclosed that the Navajo knew how to spin and weave long before they settled in the Southwest, for archaeologists have found scraps of cotton cloth in ancient caves along with other Navajo artifacts thousands of years old. Then, too, the looms of the Navajo were entirely different from those of the Pueblo. The looms the Navajo used were upright and portable, the same type of loom they use today. Navajo women made up their designs as they went along. No two rugs or blankets were exactly alike. In fact, Navajo women were, and still are, considered masters of the art of weaving.

The Navajo were well formed and lighter in color than most Indians. The women were straight, comely, and respected by the male members of the tribe. They escaped much of the hard work alloted to the women of other tribes.

The mother was the head of the family. The father, however, represented the family in public and ceremonial rites. The husband showed his respect for his mother-in-law by not speaking to her. In turn, the wife avoided her mother-in-law.

The Navajo were an adventurous people. Unlike their neighbors, the Pueblo, who built large adobe dwellings that accommodated several families, the Navajo liked to live in small clusters of related families, with their hogans in isolated spots.

When out hunting, they often came in contact with other tribes; and, when possible, they stole the other tribe's food. It is said the Navajo had a way of taking what they wanted and leaving the rest. They did not think of it as stealing. This land belonged to them. They had the right to take what they could use.

They were natural hunters. By the time a boy was seven or eight years old, he was taught how to fight, dodge arrows, dive into icy water, and roll in the snow. As he grew older, he was taught how to run during the hottest part of the day with a mouthful of water he dared not spit out until the run was over. He was then made to vomit and take a sweat bath.

When Navajo boys grew into young manhood and had

learned to look out for themselves, they sometimes were allowed to take their first smoke; and if they had excelled in some activity, they were given a new name.

Those who wanted to become fine hunters were taught how to make bows and arrows and how to shoot them. They were taught how to make and use a knife. They seldom burdened themselves with excess food when they hunted. A few wild seeds or jerked meat in the leather pouches that hung from their belts were all that was necessary. Sometimes they carried a few dried yucca leaves or fruit that had a sweet taste and could be eaten raw or dried in the sun. As a rule, they managed to catch enough game to sustain them.

The young men who wanted to become medicine men also started young. They generally were taught the art of sand painting by an elder who was no longer active. They were also taught how to use herbs and how to heal and bless.

The young girls were taught at an early age how to spin, dye, and weave the fibers of the cotton plant into colorful blankets, what herbs to gather for the cooking pots, and how to prepare game.

The Navajo were a happy people until white men invaded their sacred country. In 1540 Francisco Vásquez de Coronado and several hundred of his Spanish conquistadors crossed the Rio Grande and followed the western slope of the Sacramento Mountains northward until they reached Pueblo and Navajo land. They were in search of the seven fabled cities of Cíbola, where the streets supposedly were paved with gold.

2. The Invaders

The Navajo did not know what to think of these bearded white men, wearing gilded helmets and breastplates, who rode into their country on huge four-legged animals. The strangers carried menacing-looking weapons (crossbows and battle-axes).

Nor did the Navajo know what to think of the hundreds of sheep, cattle, and goats that followed along behind. They had never seen such men or animals. They kept their distance and watched curiously when the Mexican-Spanish Indians who were with the invaders killed and cooked a goat before making camp for the night. The more they watched, the more they realized the use that could be made of these tame animals and looked upon them with envy. Surely, the gods had sent them for some good purpose.

The Spaniards were also surprised at what they saw. The Navajos' colorful cotton blankets; leather garments; medicine pouches; arrow quivers decorated with blue stones, shells, and feathers told them that these people were a peaceful as well as an intelligent tribe. Yet the Spanish took advantage of them. They offered to trade the Navajo worthless glass beads for beautiful blue turquoise stones, then rode their huge Andalusian horses through Navajo fields of corn, beans, squash, and melons. After helping themselves, they rode away without as much as thank-you—leaving only trampled fields behind.

Angered by such treatment, the Navajo shot poisoned arrows at the retreating army. The arrows could not penetrate the metal armor, but they succeeded in knocking the leader, Coronado, off his horse. His soldiers managed to boost him back on, but they killed several Navajo in the skirmish before they rode away.

Coronado did not find the cities of gold; and after two years of searching, he gave up the quest in disgust and returned to Mexico, then called New Spain.

Several years later, other Spanish explorers, having heard of the blue stones, high mesas, and peaceful Indians who could be easily captured and sold as slaves, invaded Navajo land. This time the Navajo were not so friendly. They did not trust these white men, and it did not take them long to run the invaders out of their country.

In 1598 another explorer, Don Juan de Oñate, was commissioned by the government at Mexico City to lead an expedition into what is now known as New Mexico for the purpose of colonizing that part of the country. The expedition consisted of some 400 colonists, Mexican Indian servants and Franciscan missionaries. Oñate and his army, mounted and armed, preceded the long train of packmules and oxcarts laden with household goods, seeds, and fruit trees. These, in turn, were followed by thousands of horses, sheep, and goats. It was a long, wearisome journey over the rough, rocky trail Coronado and his army had blazed through the wilderness. Much of the expedition's stock strayed away or was stolen.

Navajo country lay just to the west and north of Pueblo country, and the Navajo helped themselves to the straying stock. The horses this time were mustangs, small, fast, surefooted, and somewhat wild. Such animals meant a faster means of travel, and the Navajo captured as many as they could find. They also captured sheep and goats and hid them back in treacherous valleys where the Spaniards could not find them.

The peaceful Pueblo had no way of knowing that Juan Oñate had orders to take formal possession of their country. Nor did they know that their land was to be divided into five districts, a priest assigned to each, and the villages to be given Spanish names. The Pueblo were friendly to the intruders; but before they realized what was happening, they were a conquered people, shearing sheep and weaving wool into mantas for priests and garments for Spanish grandees.

So far, the Spaniards had made only sporadic raids into Navajo country. Believing that the Navajo were Apaches because the two tribes spoke practically the same language, they found it difficult to distinguish between the warlike Apaches, who were hunters, and the *Apache de Nabahu*, who farmed their fields like the Pueblo. The name *Apache de Nabahu*, which was shortened to Navajo, meant "Apaches of the cultivated fields."

The Spaniards did not like the Navajo who, unlike the Pueblo, did not congregate in villages, where they could easily be controlled as slaves. Their ability to scatter and disappear in canyon passages made them almost impossible to capture. One friar is quoted as saying, "The Navajo are a wayward, if lovable, people that should be kept in permanent bondage." And this is what the Spaniards attempted to do.

As quickly as possible, churches and schools were erected to educate the conquered people, regardless of tribe. It is said that the missionaries were so determined to convert the Indians to their way of thinking that their children were baptized without the parents' consent and forced to study the catechism. When rebellious children refused to study, they were chained to pews until they became docile enough to be sold as slaves into wealthy Spanish families.

By 1600 some 500,000 Spanish and Mexican families, it is estimated, had settled in what was by then called New Spain. In 1606 a small town, not much more than a trading post, named Santa Fe, was founded at the foot of the Sangre de Cristo Mountains. This town would later play an important part in the lives of the Navajo.

This take-over did not set well with the Pueblos. By now they were sick and tired of being dominated by missionaries and the Spanish government. The Jamez, San Felipe, and Alameda Pueblos, joined by their arch enemies the Apaches, decided to do something about driving the Spaniards out of their country. But the plot was discovered, and the ringleaders were either hung, beaten, or imprisoned. The Indians continued to retaliate, however.

By then the conflict between the Spaniards and the Indians of the Southwest had become so grave that the Franciscan friars threatened to abandon New Spain and return to the old country.

By 1665 the little village of Santa Fe had become the capital of a far-flung dominion under Spanish rule; the City of the Holy Faith, it was called. Loaded oxcarts and herds of cattle were driven from old Mexico to Santa Fe, a four-month journey, to supply the trading posts and garrisons with the more sophisticated necessities of life that could not be found in the wilderness.

The Navajos kept to themselves. The Spaniards were their deadly enemies. They did not often go to Santa Fe. All this changed, however, in 1680, the year of the Great

Rebellion. The Pueblo, Hopi, and Apache Indians had again conspired in a common cause to drive the white enemies out of their country. This time the Spaniards and Mexicans were taken by surprise. Before they realized what was happening, churches, missions, and government buildings were being ransacked and burned, and records destroyed. Spaniards and Mexicans were killed by the hundreds. It is said that the blood of priests, missionaries, and government authorities flowed freely and that those who were not killed fled for their lives before the horde of angry Indians.

Within a few days, the Pueblo had taken over the governor's palace and the adobe homes of wealthy Spaniards. Here, for the next twelve years, they lived in peace.

The Navajo did not join in this rebellion. They were not warriors as such. They did not like to kill. Fearing the Spaniards would return, they took refuge in the canyons until the turmoil was over, then gathered up the wandering horses, sheep, and goats and added them to their ever increasing herds.

In 1692 General de Vargas, explorer and conquistador, was sent by the Spanish government to reconquer the so-called City of the Holy Faith for the Spanish Crown. It was practically a bloodless battle. The Pueblo left Santa Fe and returned to their adobe dwellings. Many of the Jamez Pueblo sent their daughters into Navajo country for safety, which resulted in many intermarriages.

Keenly aware of the constant Spanish threat, several bands of Navajo abandoned their homes in northwestern New Mexico during the 1700s and drifted westward over the sandy, windswept desert to the Canyon de Chelly region, now northeastern Arizona, but still within the confines of their four sacred mountains.

Bounded on the north by the San Juan River, the

country was covered with dwarf piñon, gnarled juniper, high mesas, and steep rocky cliffs of irregular shapes and forms. On the south it was bounded by a desert covered with the succulent, fleshy leaves of the prickly pear and giant saguaro. On the west it was bounded by the Little Colorado River and the Hopi Indians; on the east, by Apache and Pueblo country and by the Spaniards.

Near the eastern border of what is now Arizona was the awesome Canyon de Chelly, pronounced *de shay*. The river de Chelly and its tributaries wound a treacherous course, over quicksand in places, through vertical walls ranging in depth from 1,000 to 30 feet, supplying the numerous year-round springs and fertile valleys with crystal clear water. The gradual concentration of various Navajo groups in this region led to the establishment of several settlements near these everflowing springs.

It was a wild untamed country, harsh and unrelenting at times; but now that the Navajo had fast, well-trained mustangs for travel, hunting, and raiding, as well as sheep and goats for food and wool, they were more independent. Embraced by their four sacred mountains, they sang their prayer songs and danced their ceremonial dances for a time without fear.

There were no white men in this area other than an occasional fur trapper who had the good sense not to invade their sacred land.

In time the Navajo spread out over the entire desert area. The groups that remained in the Mt. Taylor region became friendly with the Spanish friars, who often provided them with food. This friendship ceased, however, when the friars insisted that they become converted. Only a few Navajo spoke Spanish; but they managed to make the friars understand that while they had no enmity towards them, Spanish ways were not their ways. Spanish gods were not their gods.

Soon after this, the Franciscans gave up the mission and moved on. However, the Mt. Taylor Navajo, who continued to trade with the Spaniards, were branded as "enemy Navajo" by other groups of Navajo; and the raids for slaves, sheep, and horses continued. Prisoners were taken on both sides. The hostilities between the Navajo and the Spaniards increased, especially in the desert area.

During the hostilities between the Navajo and the Spanish in the Southwest, a revolutionary war was being fought in the East. The American colonists, determined to rule themselves, were fighting for their independence, and they won. The united colonies declared themselves free and independent of Great Britain on July 4, 1776. Before that, however, the Continental Congress had adopted a policy to push the eastern Indians westward and to regulate commerce with the Indian tribes. This did not apply to the Indians of the Southwest, who were under Spanish rule.

The Navajo had no knowledge of the vast stretch of land east of the Rockies or of its problems; and had they known, it would not have meant anything to them. They were too busy fighting a war of their own. Moving to the Canyon de Chelly area had not helped the situation. The slave markets in Santa Fe were hungry for captured slaves, and Navajo women and children were easy prey as they tended their sheep in small valleys or near an oasis on the desert. Women and children from ages six to 16 were bringing $200 each on the slave market, which encouraged more and more raiders to invade Navajo country.

Little by little, the Navajo learned to become more warlike. In an effort to get back their own people who had been stolen, they raided Spanish and Mexican settlements at every opportunity; and while there, they stole as many sheep, horses, and goats as possible.

In fact, when once the Navajos turned warriors, they were good warriors. Their depredations reached such a pitch that the Spaniards claimed their economy was in jeopardy.

Thousands of Navajo were killed or captured during this period. Yet through it all, the majority of them continued to speak their own language and retain their own culture.

3. The Mexican Revolution

THE UNITED STATES government, having won its freedom from Great Britain, turned its attention toward the West. One of the first and most important transactions of the new government was the Louisiana Purchase, which led to the westward movement and in time to the pushing back of the red men from their lands.

This vast tract of land west of the Mississippi River, consisting of some 820,000 square miles, included the states of Missouri, Arkansas, parts of North Dakota, South Dakota, Colorado, and nearly all of Kansas, Nebraska, and Oklahoma. After much debating and wrangling, France ceded it to the United States April 1, 1803, for a sum exceeding 15 million dollars, less than four cents an acre.

During this period the Spaniards continued their slave raids against the Navajo. In 1803 a troop of Spanish soldiers thrust their bayonets into the frightened flesh of over a hundred Navajo women and children hiding in the Canyon del Muerto, a branch of the Canyon de Chelly, until all were killed.

There were about as many Mexicans as there were Spaniards in the Southwest at that time, and the political trend of the Spanish rulers disturbed the more conservative

17

Mexican leaders. Determined to obtain their freedom from such an autocratic government, the Mexican leaders combined forces in 1813 and started a revolution that lasted until 1821, when they won control of the government.

While the New Mexicans were waging a war of independence from Spanish rule, the Navajo were free to continue their unorganized raids, which seldom involved more than a few bands. Infuriated by their treatment at the hands of the Spaniards, they vented their hatred by raiding and plundering everything in sight in an effort to recapture some of their own people and add to their ever-increasing herds of sheep and horses.

The beginning of Mexican rule in the Southwest marked a period of intrigue and corruption. Gambling was made legal, and saloons were opened on the Plaza, the public square of Santa Fe. The first territorial governor was killed, as were those that followed. Faced with the same raiding and plundering problems, the governors attempted to solve them in the same way and were promptly eliminated.

By then Santa Fe had become the capital of New Mexico territory and a center of trading power. The governor's palace was restored and became the scene of gay festivities attended by Spanish grandees, outlaws, aristocrats, gamblers, adventurers, and courtesans alike. On the Plaza, colonels, majors, and captains gambled, as did lawyers, doctors, priests, traders, outlaws and oxcart drivers.

The Plaza was also the scene of public spectacles, such as the head of an ex-governor being paraded on a stick, a public flogging, or a prisoner locked in the stocks cursing his fate. Here, too, friendly Indians, mainly Pueblos, could exchange their wares for food or trinkets.

The Plaza never lacked excitement, especially when a caravan of heavily loaded freight wagons and packmules laden with merchandise arrived from Missouri. The Spaniards had refused to permit trade between the territory and the United States, but the Mexicans welcomed it. Most of the merchants in Santa Fe were wholesale dealers for a vast territory and were always in need of new items to sell.

Anglo-Americain commerce with Mexico was important. White Anglo-American traders could make an enormous profit in transporting household goods, food, guns, liquor, and trinkets across the 900 miles of grassy plains between Missouri and the Rocky Mountains, over the Santa Fe Trail. The trail had been blazed in 1812 by William Becknell, who later became known as the Father of the Santa Fe Trail, and it was used until the coming of the railroad in 1880.

It was a dangerous expedition in those early days. Even though the traders were armed, old flintlock rifles carried only one shot, which was not too effective against skilled warriors with poisoned arrows, knives, and lances. Only a few expeditions were made before 1824, when commerce was established between Mexico and the United States.

From then on, long caravans of wheeled vehicles, mainly Conestoga freight wagons, made their way over the Santa Fe Trail to the Raton Pass, where they turned south and traveled a circuitous route to Santa Fe. One caravan alone, containing 3,500 wagons, 4,500 men, 40,000 oxen, and 1,000 mules, is said to have hauled 16,000,000 pounds of goods annually.

At first, the traders had very little trouble with hostile Indians. This condition did not last long, however. Instead of establishing a friendly relationship with the Indians over whose land they crossed, they wantonly killed the Indians in cold blood because some detached band had committed an outrage on an isolated settlement. This, of

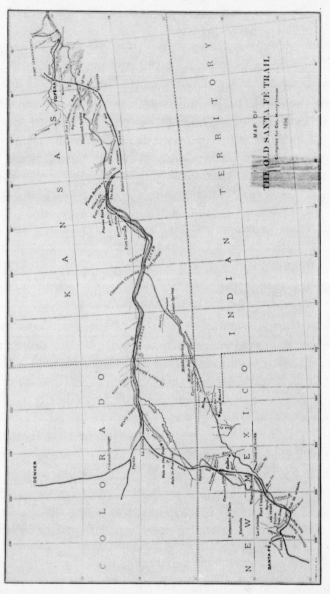

The Old Santa Fe Trail. From Henry Inman, *The Old Santa Fe Trail* (1897).

20

course, enraged the once friendly Indians, until the United States government was forced to send several companies of cavalry to escort the caravans across the plains.

The transfer of government from Spanish to Mexican rule had little effect upon the Navajo. By then their flocks of sheep had increased to tens of thousands. Their horses had multiplied to more than 20,000, and this increased their raiding power. These raids seldom involved more than a few groups in need of food or material goods, and many times these necessities were incidental to the capturing of slaves or getting back some of their own people. By now, raiding had become an established means of livelihood. The War Chiefs often paid little attention to the advice of the more peaceful headmen.

Expeditions were launched to invade Navajo country for the purpose of exterminating the whole tribe, but these too failed. The Navajo hid in caves or on high ledges and dropped rocks on the troops as they made their way through the winding passageways.

The first colonization in New Mexican territory by the United States government was at Taos in 1830 after the Bureau of Indian Affairs was founded in 1824 by the War Department.

The first migration of Anglo-Americans from the East did not occur until 1843, however, when a train of covered wagons piled high with household belongings crossed the Missouri River and headed west. The wagons, called prairie schooners, were not quite as large as the Conestoga freight wagons, but they were as sturdily made and caulked so that they, too, could float on swollen rivers and streams in rainy weather.

Navajo country was some distance from Santa Fe. Only a few Navajo had ever seen white Anglo-Americans or guns.

The whole country was changing, however. In 1843 a portait painter in the East, Samuel F. B. Morse, invented an electrical device that could send messages over a wire. This was a great step forward in communication. It was several years, though, before the singing wire, as the Indians called the telegraph, reached the West.

Transportation by rail was still in the experimental stage, but the significant part rails could play in linking the East to the West was becoming more and more apparent. Several men of affluence and power in Washington had already won from Congress federal grants to be used for the building of railroads.

In the meantime the Anglo-Americans who had settled in Texas not only were unhappy about Mexicans' stealing their stock, but they were also concerned about the southern boundary line of their territory. The Mexican government claimed the Nueces River was the southern line. The Americans insisted it was the Rio Grande.

This dispute disturbed newly elected U.S. President Polk, especially when the Mexicans issued an order to evict all American settlers in Upper California and to prohibit further migration of Americans to that part of the country.

In an effort to negotiate a treaty over the disputed land in Texas and a possible purchase of Upper California, President Polk sent John Slidell, a diplomat, to Mexico. The president felt certain that an offer of $25,000,000 for a stretch of land Mexico had never populated and had difficulty in controlling would be welcomed. If Mexico agreed to the sale of Upper California, American expansion could go unchecked to the Pacific ocean.

To the president's surprise, the Mexicans considered the offer an insult and a veiled threat to take over all their land north of the Rio Grande, and they sent troops to the Nueces River to stop the Americans. President Polk considered this an invasion of American soil and declared war on Mexico May 11, 1846. He then called for an army of 50,000 volunteers to fight against Mexico. Brigadier General Stephen W. Kearny was appointed commander of this "Army of the West."

4. The Army of the West

During the summer of 1846, General Kearny left Fort Leavenworth, Kansas, with a force of some 1,600 troops to occupy the province of New Mexico at Santa Fe, which had been seized and declared a part of the United States. His mission was not only to establish a military government at Santa Fe, but also to push on to California, where the war with Mexico was raging.

His force consisted of two batteries of artillery under the command of Major Clark, three squadrons of the First United States Dragoons under the command of Major Sumner, the First Regiment of Missouri Cavalry under the command of Colonel Doniphan, and two companies of infantry under the command of Captain Aubrey. Several army wagons loaded with provisions and a hundred or more cattle trailed along behind.

It took 50 days of continued march to cross the 900 miles of prairies darkened with great herds of buffalo, deserts where water was scarce, and the treacherous Raton Pass. It is said the "Army of the West" was composed of as fine material as any body of troops in the field. The entire corps consisted mainly of young men from that part of the country.

When the army reached the Cimarron Crossing of the Arkansas River, July 20, they made camp on Mexican soil about eight miles below Bent's Fort. From there General Kearny dispatched Colonel Doniphan with his command to join General Zachary Taylor in the northern part of old Mexico. Other officers and men were dispatched to various posts where they were needed most. The general then established a camp near Bent's Fort before he and his men proceeded on to Santa Fe.

On August 18, 1846, General Kearny, almost without resistance, took possession of Santa Fe and the entire area. Charles Bent, of Bent's Fort, was appointed governor. Other offices were filled with Americans and Mexicans loyal to the United States.

The general had no more than set up headquarters, however, when he was besieged by delegations of Pueblo and Zuñi Indians, Mexican ranchers, and American civilians, demanding protection from marauding Indians, mostly Navajo.

It was difficult for the general to fight a war with Mexico and the Navajo at the same time, but he could not ignore the demands for protection. Standing on the Plaza, one block east of the governor's palace, he explained to the crowd gathered there that he had come not as an enemy, but as a protector and that he intended to put a stop to the Indian raids.

He did not immediately organize a campaign against the Navajo, however. He first wanted to meet with some of their chiefs and, if possible, get them to sign a peace treaty so that he could get on with winning the Mexican War.

General Kearny, like the Spanish and Mexican officials before him, did not understand that there was no acknowledged head chief of the Navajo nation, or central government to deal with, that the Navajo were divided into many bands or groups with a chieftain at the head of each, or that a treaty signed by one or two chiefs did not bind the chiefs of other groups.

Before the general could arrange a meeting with several Navajo chiefs, he received word that California had declared its independence of Mexico. The message also informed him that Captain John C. Frémont, who was in California with a topographical expedition, had taken command of the rebel forces and enlisted them in the United States Army and that Commodore Robert F. Stockton had seized the Mexican stronghold at Los Angeles and had issued a proclamation declaring himself governor of California, naming Captain Frémont as military commandant.

Upon receipt of this report, General Kearny dispatched a messenger to Colonel Doniphan, ordering him to delay his move to old Mexico and proceed with his regiment to Navajo country to stop the depredations there. He himself would press on to California.

After receiving this order, October 11, 1846, Colonel Doniphan organized his campaign. Winter had set in by then, and his troops were not equipped with enough warm clothing, blankets, or tents for a prolonged march. He dispatched an order to Major Gilpin, however, to move his troops up the Chama River to Abiquiu and from there to Bear Springs. Gilpin was to chastise hostile Indians along the way and to send out word for the chiefs to meet him at Bear Springs.

By October 14, Major Gilpin and his troops had managed to advance a hundred miles through deep snow. A packmule had died of exhaustion and slipped over the brink of a chasm along the way, but the major and his troops had finally made it to Bear Springs.

In the meantime, Colonel Doniphan and his troops

went up the Puerco River of the west and spread out over the country, gathering up Navajo leaders as they moved along. Major Gilpin with a delegation of several chiefs and warriors was waiting for him at the springs.

After Colonel Doniphan had explained the purpose of the meeting and the chieftains had pow-wowed among themselves, Zarcillas Largo wanted to know why they no longer were permitted to fight their sworn enemies for what belonged to them. The Mexicans had been their enemies long before they were the white man's enemies.

For a moment Colonel Doniphan was nonplussed. He was new at dealing with Indians, and he too believed that the signing of a treaty by a few Navajo Chiefs was binding on the tribe as a whole. He attempted to explain, however, that if the Navajo were permitted to continue fighting and raiding the Mexicans, it would not be long until they would be fighting the Americans, which, of course, could not be allowed. He then warned them that if they did not stop their raids and return the stolen stock and the captives, the United States government would be forced to make war against them.

After the chieftains had again pow-wowed among themselves, Zarcillas agreed to stop raiding the Mexicans and return the stolen stock and the captives. The headmen then made their marks on a piece of paper they could not read and disappeared into the canyons. The troops returned to their posts.

By the time the treaty reached Santa Fe, however, the Navajo signers of the treaty realized they had agreed to give up everything and receive nothing in return. No promise had been made by the Anglo-Americans for the return of the Navajos' stock or captured members. The more the Navajo pondered this situation, the more incensed they became. The deep-seated hatred for all white men smoldering within them again burst into flame. They had been tricked.

They not only ignored the treaty, but renewed their raids until the incursions reached such a high point that the United States government thought it necessary to send another expedition into Navajo country in an effort to establish peace.

On September 10, 1847, Major H. T. Walker, with a battalion of Missouri volunteers left Santa Fe to invade Navajo country. He was equipped with provisions for two months and a small detachment of artillery. Determined to humble the Navajo and give them a good chastisement, the troops set off in high spirits. When the expedition of 140 men reached the eastern entrance of the Canyon de Chelly, Major Walker decided to penetrate the canyon; but after proceeding some six or seven miles without encountering any Indians, he realized the danger of going farther and ordered his men to backtrack out of the gorge before they were trapped. They reached Santa Fe October 13, 1847. A short time later, however, several Navajo headmen, realizing another campaign would be launched against them, appeared and offered to treat for peace. A council was called, and the Navajo chieftains agreed to keep the peace. Quiet reigned throughout the remainder of that year. By spring, however, the Navajo renewed their raids.

The Treaty of Guadalupe-Hidalgo, signed February 2, 1848, ended the war with Mexico, but not with the Indians. The United States acquired the land it had so eagerly sought, a land of vast distances, broad flat deserts, and high mountains, from which streams of cascading water tumbled into fertile valleys. No one knew just how many Indians resided in this vast territory, but it was estimated that there were at least 300,000, most of them hostile. Therefore, it was easier to win this war than to maintain the peace that followed. No one realized at that time that acquisition of this new territory would be instrumental in dividing the nation into factions and result in a civil war. Neither did Colonel E. W. Newby, the new commander of New Mexico. He had sent two expeditions into Navajo country and succeeded in negotiating a treaty with a few chiefs. It did not stop the raiding of other bands, however. They continued their raids with renewed zeal.

It was learned later that many of these raids were deliberately instigated by Mexican ranchers, not only to obtain stock for their own herds, but also to capture women and children and to throw suspicion on the Navajo.

At the same time, the United States was faced with a new problem. Gold had been discovered in California. By the spring of 1849, gold-seekers from the East were swarming across the plains and mountains by the thousands.

By then the Bureau of Indian Affairs had been formed and became a part of the Department of the Interior. James S. Calhoun, a veteran of the Mexican war, was appointed the first Indian agent to New Mexico territory July 22, 1849. A man of vision and common sense, he decided to study the situation of the Navajo before taking any action. He learned to his surprise that although they were troublesome and stole livestock, they did not destroy settlements, homes, or fields when they made a raid, nor were they dangerous warriors unless forced to defend themselves. He also learned that Mexican raiders not only destroyed settlements, homes, and fields when raiding, but also captured women and children to sell as slaves.

Agent Calhoun, working in accord with the new military governor, Colonel John M. Washington, also learned that the Navajo considered the bluecoats poor soldiers and the Anglo-American officers weaklings.

On August 22, 1849, Colonel Washington, with seven companies of soldiers, marched against the Navajo. Antonio Sandoval, chief of one enemy group of the Mt. Taylor region, acted as their guide and interpreter. When the soldiers reached the valley of the Tunicha, a tributary of the San Juan, they camped for the night near fields of Navajo corn and a herd of sheep. Since forage for their animals had been scarce and the troops were hungry for fresh meat, they helped themselves.

While they were eating and resting, several headmen appeared to take council with the new governor. Colonel Washington's message was brief. He informed the Navajo that he planned to chastise them for their disregard of the Doniphan and Newby treaties. In defense, the chiefs, Largo, Archulets, and Narbona, explained that although there were some "bad" Navajo, over whom they had no control, the majority wanted peace and would return the stock they had stolen.

While the message was being interpreted, a soldier spotted a horse he thought to be his and demanded its return. When the Navajo refused to surrender the animal, Colonel Washington directed the soldiers to take possession of the horse or any loose horse they could capture. While the attempt to capture one was going on, the Navajo fled and were fired upon. Chief Narbona was mortally wounded in the skirmish, and several Navajo warriors were killed.

The command moved on and reached the Canyon de Chelly, where Colonel Washington hoped to make contact with all the chiefs; but the Navajo had fled. Fearing the Anglo-Americans, they had set fire to their hogans and disappeared with their sheep, goats, and horses into the labyrinth of passageways.

Several days later, three chiefs called on the governor

to sign a treaty, in which they agreed to stay on their own land and to return the stolen stock and human captives.

Conditions were not as peaceful as they seemed, however. The majority of the Navajo were filled with resentment. The Anglo-Americans had not only invaded their land, but had also picketed their horses in Navajo corn fields and killed Navajo sheep and their most respected chief, Narbona.

Colonel Washington, believing he had intimidated them, was elated with his success. The Indian agent Calhoun was disgusted not only by the colonel's lack of control, but also with the mismanagement of the whole campaign.

In the meantime, the Navajo whose chiefs had signed the treaty went about gathering up the stolen stock. Before they could deliver it or the human captives, a trader from the Zuñi area informed them that several hundred Mexican settlers, along with a few Anglo-Americans, were forming a volunteer army of vigilantes to wipe out the whole tribe. Frightened by such rumors and stunned at the prospect of their flocks' being destroyed and their women and children sold into slavery, the Navajo once again went on the warpath.

By November, 1849, the agent Calhoun suggested to the new military governor, John Munroe, that the most effective way to stop such vicious rumors was to force the traders to buy a license and to restrict their territory.

Two weeks later, Governor Munroe posted a notice to the effect that henceforth all traders dealing with Indians of any tribe had to purchase a license to work in New Mexico and that a license would be granted only to citizens of the United States after they had posted a bond of $5,000 or less and agreed to refrain from selling firearms, powder, lead, or ammunition to Indians. The notice also made it plain that each applicant had to state which tribe of Indians he planned to deal with.

By March 1850, a delegation of New Mexicans, headed by one Manuel Chaves, requested authority to organize an army of volunteers to march against the Navajo. In return for their services, they asked the government to furnish them with mules, rifles, and sufficient ammunition to conduct a sucessful campaign, as well as to grant them the disposal of all captives, animal or human. They also wanted the assurance that they would be subject only to the civil government and not to the military government.

As much as he needed relief from Indian raids, the agent Calhoun explained that he had no authority to permit them to form an army of volunteers or to issue firearms. The commander of the Ninth Military Department had sole control over such matters. Permission for such an exploit was, of course, not granted.

5. Fort Defiance

WHILE THE NAVAJO continued to raid white settlements, the United States government at Washington, D.C., wondered how best to organize the vast stretch of wilderness, including the present state of Arizona and part of Colorado, that had been declared the Territory of New Mexico on September 9, 1850. The main problem was what to do with the thousands of Indians who lived on this land.

The Committee of Indian Affairs was working on a bill to present to Congress, recommending the removal of Indian tribes from the more valuable regions to less productive land, where they could be controlled and taught how to farm for a living. The secretary of war was seeking ways to strengthen frontier defenses and reduce expenses.

On March 4, 1851, James S. Calhoun was installed as the first civil governor of New Mexico. His position also included the duties of superintendent of Indian affairs in that territory. Colonel Munroe, the military governor, was replaced by Colonel Edwin V. Sumner, commander of the Ninth Military Department, on April 1, 1851. His instructions were to reduce expenses, protect the settlers from the

The Canyon de Chelly. Its walls range in depth from 1,000 to 30 feet. Courtesy the Mullarky Photo Shop, Gallup, N.M.

Indians, and work in accord with the new civil governor and superintendent of Indian affairs, James S. Calhoun.

Colonel Sumner reached Santa Fe on July 5, 1851. After withdrawing the garrisons at Las Vegas, Raydo, and Albuquerque, he left Santa Fe with a company of soldiers, equipped for a two-month journey into Navajo land.

The troops saw very few Navajo until they reached the Canyon Bonito that nestled between redstone hills some 15 miles south of the Canyon de Chelly and about three miles west of what is now the eastern boundary of Arizona. The Canyon Bonito was not much more than a half mile long and a hundred yards wide. A deep, clear pool of water, fed by two springs that overflowed into a lively stream, ran along the length of the canyon. A shrine made of stones had recently been erected near the pool. Bright blue stones and white shells had been dropped into the water, evidently as a penance for some sin, a blessing, or a prayer.

While the troops rested, Colonel Sumner sent a message to the Navajo chieftains in the vicinity to meet him at the springs to talk things over. When no one showed up the next morning, the troops moved on to the Canyon de Chelly. As they neared the entrance to this colossal gorge and stood looking down into its awful depths, they were amazed not only at its depth, but also at the ancient cliff dwellings perched on ledges 600 to 700 feet above the floor of the canyon. As far as they could see, there were no means of ascent other than a few faint imprints of toeholds embedded in the sheer rock walls.

As Colonel Sumner and his men moved cautiously down into the mouth of the gaping hole, Navajo men, women, and children could be seen high above their heads as they moved along. And although the ledges were not as high as the cliff dwellings, they were too high for gunshots or arrows to reach them. Taunting voices could be heard, though, reverberating from wall to wall.

The troops stopped to satisfy their hunger when they reached a small orchard tucked back in a valley; then they moved on. It was such a dangerous undertaking that the colonel, after consulting with his men, decided not to risk their lives by penetrating the canyon any farther. He had seen enough, however, to convince him that a garrison should be established in the heart of Navajo country and that the Canyon Bonito would be an ideal location for such a fort. On September 18, 1851, he issued a special order for a military post to be erected in the Bonito Hills, to be named Fort Defiance, an appropriate name in his opinion.

The fact that it would be 70 miles northwest of Zuñi and 270 miles from the Rio Grande at Albuquerque and that it would be dangerous and difficult for supply trains to reach, did not deter him. A fort so near the Navajos' stronghold should check their incursions into the white man's country and help to enforce the treaty.

When finished, Fort Defiance consisted of a long row of log barracks, officers' quarters, a log and mud warehouse, stables for the regimental mounts, a parade ground, and forage pasture. There were no stockades, trenches, or blockhouses. The sandstone walls rising high on each side of the canyon would be their protection.

Fort Defiance did not have the immediate effect Colonel Sumner had hoped for. In fact, it had just the opposite result. The Navajo resented the intrusion of the soldiers on their land, and they became more hostile than ever. Several campaigns were launched against them from the fort, but most of them were failures.

After that, applications to raise an army of volunteers

to war against the Navajo again poured into the superintendent's office. Calhoun was in favor of raising such an army, but Colonel Sumner was against a nonmilitary expedition moving into Navajo country. There had been considerable disagreement between the superintendent of Indian affairs and the military commander, who did not always see eye to eye.

This lack of cooperation between the civil government and the military bothered Colonel Sumner. On November 20, 1851, he sent a message to the adjutant general of the army, which asserted, in part, that this two-hundred-year-old war between the Mexicans and the Navajo would probably continue indefinitely unless conditions were changed. Sumner did, however, expect to reap advantages from the establishment of Fort Defiance. He expected the fort to cramp the Navajos' movements but feared that a civilian war would disrupt the progress initiated by the fort's construction. He urged that his troops be allowed to protect the Navajo from the invasion of a volunteer army of Mexican and American settlers.

The General's answer to this message instructed Colonel Sumner to act in accord with the Superintendent of Indian affairs, in all negotiations.

During the winter of 1851–52, a delegation of Navajo leaders came to Santa Fe to consult with Calhoun. He told them, however, that the troops at Fort Defiance could and would prevent them from raising their crops in the spring if they did not remain at peace and that he would do all he could to keep the white settlers from invading their country.

This talk with the superintendent of Indian affairs impressed the chiefs; and after a treaty was signed, Calhoun distributed over a thousand dollars' worth of calico, brass wire, tobacco, and other items dear to the Navajos' heart.

Fort Defiance at Canyon Bonito, New Mexico. From an engraving of a drawing by Lt. Col. J. H. Eaton, USA. Courtesy of the General Services Administration, National Archives and Records Service, Washington, D.C. (U.S. Signal Corps photo no. 111-SC-98806)

Fort Defiance, Indian Agency, Arizona, today. Photograph by Ben Wittick. Courtesy Museum of New Mexico, Santa Fe, N.M.

It seemed for a time that Fort Defiance had accomplished what the armies of Spain, Mexico, and the United States had failed to accomplish in the past.

After Calhoun's death in 1853, William C. Lane, a veteran of the Mexican War, was appointed to take his place. Lane's policy was one of appeasement. He believed it was cheaper to feed the Navajo than to fight them. He also agreed with the government's resolution to send the Indians to some isolated reservation. However, since the government had not had time to survey the land for such purposes, he negotiated as many treaties as possible.

In the meantime, Antonio Sandoval once again was spreading rumors that plans were being made to exterminate the Navajo. Hearing of these rumors, Lane sent gifts for the commander at Fort Defiance to hand out, hoping to allay any fears Sandoval might have roused. This gesture would probably have helped, had not a Mexican sheepherder in the Zuñi area been mortally wounded, a son kidnapped, and his sheep stolen.

Hearing of the incident and the dangers involved, the superintendent Lane sent word to the territorial secretary to demand the return of the murderer, the kidnapped boy, and the stolen sheep. When informed of these demands, Jasin, a Zuñi chief, explained that the murder and the theft had been committed by a band over which he had no control. There was nothing he could do about it.

Lane refused to accept such an excuse. He hoped to be elected a delegate to Congress and felt that a strict attitude toward the Navajo would help him win this election. He sent back word that if his demands were not met within a week, he would declare war on all the Navajo.

When a week passed and his demands had not been met, he got in touch with Colonel Sumner. Inasmuch as there were only about 500 Americans in the region as opposed to some 60,000 Mexicans and 45,000 Indians, Colonel Sumner did not consider it wise to war against several thousand Navajo when only a few were involved.

Dissatisfied with Sumner's attitude, Lane ordered the commander of the fort to press demands for the surrender of the culprits, with force if necessary. Complying with this order, the commander, with Captain Henry Linn Dodge, a veteran of the Washington expedition, warned the Navajo chiefs of the Zuñi area that war was inevitable unless they complied with Lane's demands.

The Navajo not only ignored Lane's threat, but his attitude toward the Navajo had little effect on his political campaign, for he was defeated. Disgusted, he resigned his post and left Santa Fe for the States. Captain David Meriwether was appointed to finish out Lane's term of office, and Colonel Sumner was relieved of his duties by General Garland.

David Meriwether was no stranger to the Navajo. As an Indian trader, he had visited Santa Fe and the surrounding country many times. Upon taking office, he had a talk with several chiefs in the Zuñi area, extended amnesty, and so settled the matter.

As he became more acquainted with the source of the trouble between the red men and the white, Meriwether sought some way to end the conflicts. "If the Navajo would agree to give up a strip of their land bodering the white settlements to act as a 'buffer zone,' it would be easier for the military to enforce the intercourse laws," he reasoned. The Navajo would have to be paid for the land, of course, which would be in the form of annuities; and the value of the property the Indians had stolen could be deducted from them.

The Navajo refused to give up a strip of their land to act as a "buffer zone," and the matter was dropped. To help

keep the peace, Meriwether appointed Captain Henry Linn
Dodge civil agent to the Navajo. Fort Defiance was to be
his headquarters.

Unlike most soldiers, Captain Dodge sympathized
with the Navajo. He believed he could serve them best by
establishing his headquarters in their country, and he made
his residence near Bear Springs. He next hired a blacksmith
and a Mexican assistant, who also did some sliversmithing,
to teach the Navajo ironforging. He then took off unafraid
on a tour of Navajo country to get better acquainted with
the land and the people and found, to his surprise, that the
Navajo had good-sized pastures in spots and that their
gardens, corn fields, and peach orchards were well tended.

After completing his tour of the country, he journeyed
to Santa Fe on August 3, 1853, with 100 Navajo chieftains.
A council was called; and when the Navajo assembled, he
explained that he intended to keep the peace between the
red men and the white by hearing what the white men had
to say with one ear and what the Navajo had to say with
the other ear. Then he would weigh what both had said and
make an impartial decision. He warned them, however, that
once he had made up his mind, he would not change it and
that they must obey.

He then passed out medallions to the chiefs, including
a larger one to Zarcillo Largo, whom he invested with the
authority to speak for all those present. This seemed to
please the serious, strong-jawed Navajo leaders. They signed
a treaty to stay on their own land.

From then on, prospects for a better relationship between the Navajo and the white settlers along the border
seemed likely, until February 17, 1854, when it was reported
that white men were grazing sheep on Navajo land that
already was threatened with overgrazing.

When the agent Dodge complained of this intrusion,

he was informed that during the winter the district court had ruled that under the laws of Congress there was no Indian territory in New Mexico. Thus, stock raisers might graze their flocks on public domain wherever they chose.

Since the Navajo knew nothing of the law that had so recently gone into effect, there was a great deal of fighting along both the western and eastern borders of Navajo country; but the relationship at and near Fort Defiance continued to improve. Agent Dodge had gained the Navajos' friendship, confidence, and respect. Moreover, he had not only made it possible for some of the men to become expert ironworkers, but had also removed the threat of constant danger. Navajo women and children in that area could once again tend their flocks in peace. As far as the Navajo were concerned, it was still their country.

6. Tensions Mount

CONDITIONS CHANGED IN 1855. The Utes, always an aggressive tribe, were restless. Their favorite hunting grounds were being overrun by white men, and they were seeking reinforcements from their old enemies, the Navajo, to assist them in an attack on the white settlers. They begged the Navajo not to plant their crops in the spring, but to go with them on the warpath. They boasted of how, in the early fifties, before Kit Carson became their agent, they had killed hundreds of white men, women, and children and driven off their stock, which they were willing to share if the Navajo would join them.

Hearing of the Utes' plan to influence his fairly peaceful charges, the agent Dodge ordered more iron, copper wire, and a small amount of silver to keep the Navajo braves busy during the winter. Some of them, under the guidance of the blacksmith, already were making bridle rings and buckles, while others were learning how to work with silver under the guidance of Juan Ares.

The agent's report of May 2, 1855, was favorable concerning the conduct of the Navajo. "They are enjoying their peace and prosperity," he wrote the Bureau of Indian

Affairs, "and I doubt if they can be presuaded to join the Utes in an uprising."

Unable to recruit the necessary forces for an effective attack, the Utes did not go on the warpath that spring. When the snows melted, most of the Navajo were breaking ground for their crops.

During this time, the government in Washington, D.C., realizing the need for faster communication and transportation than stagecoaches or mule-drawn wagons between the East and the West, ordered the secretary of war to make a survey of all the best routes to California with a view to building a railroad.

General William T. Sherman was also interested in pushing such a project. As a young lieutenant and a West Pointer, he had arrived in California with a troop of soldiers on the old warship *Lexington* in 1847, and he had been there when gold was discovered. As the miners, gold-seekers, and drifters swarmed into California, he had watched with interest small towns and villages spring into being.

Sherman was promoted to a captaincy in 1850 and transferred to St. Louis, Missouri. He did not return to California until 1855. The threat of an all-out war was a constant danger, however. Since the Indians refused to live up to the treaties they had signed with an X, the gold-seeking whites thought no more of killing an Indian for land than of killing an animal for food.

General Sherman favored concentrating the Indians in New Mexico on reservations some distance from white settlements, with military establishments nearby.

General Sherman's brother, John, a senator from Ohio, wrote to him asking his advice regarding the Indian situation in California and the prospects of building a railroad through such rough and hostile country. General Sherman's report was honest, but not encouraging. It said in effect that conditions in California were anything but settled; that white settlements were being pushed forward more than the extent of the white population; that the Indians were being expelled from their homes without the right to protest; and that, provoked beyond endurance, they had no alternative but to steal, rob, and kill when necessary.

The general then advised his brother that he could do himself proud as a public servant by aiding California which, so far, had been poorly represented, he believed the country was in need of a railroad from East to West. Such a railroad, however, would cost over $2,000,000 and take 10 years to build. What was needed more urgently were good wagon and stagecoach roads so people could travel faster and safer. These roads would require not only good roads, but military posts along the routes and resting places every 15 to 20 miles, and guards to ride shotgun. The building of a railroad through mountainous and hostile country was the work of giants and Uncle Sam was the only giant big enough to tackle such a huge project.

Concerned over the prospect of a civil war, General Sherman resigned his post in 1859 and returned East. It was not long, though, before work was begun on a stagecoach road to the West. The Overland Mail Service, which ran a stagecoach between San Antonio, Texas, and San Diego, California, agreed to establish a stage line from San Francisco to the Missouri River. As General Sherman had recommended, the road was well guarded.

The stage line did not pass through Arizona for very long, however. It stopped when the War between the States broke out. There were no men left to guard or run it.

During this time, the Navajo had been going along on a fairly even keel. The Utes had settled down, and the country, except in a few instances, was as peaceful as a new

General William T. Sherman. Courtesy of the General Services Administration, National Archives and Records Service, Washington, D.C. (U.S. Signal Corps photo no. 111-BA-2027: Brady Collection.)

territory could be. Then in July 1858, the new post commander at Fort Defiance, Major T. L. Brooks, set aside a large grazing pasture for the regimental mounts; the Navajo had been using it for hundreds of years. He not only set it aside but told the Navajo leaders that the land no longer belonged to them and that any of their horses or sheep found on this land would be killed.

Such an order infuriated the Navajo. They refused to

obey. The next day, some 60 horses and over 100 sheep that had been left in the field lay dead. They had been shot. In the skirmish that followed, a Negro slave belonging to Major Brooks was accidentally killed. Major Brooks immediately demanded the surrender of the one responsible for the slave's death. Manuelito, a Navajo chief in the vicinity, attempted to settle the matter in Navajo tradition by paying "blood money." This was accomplished by dragging a Mexican slave to death and offering the body to the bluecoats. This offer was refused. Several assaults were launched against the Navajo without results other than the killing of a few innocent Navajo women and children while they were tending their sheep.

A few days later, a couple of Navajo chieftains arrived at the fort and signed a treaty to stay on their own land. Other Navajo bands continued their forays from Zuñi to the San Juan River.

In April 1859, gold was discovered in Colorado. Almost overnight thousands of covered wagons set out for this area. Most of this land was considered Ute country, and once again the Utes went on the warpath, plundering and killing the invading white squatters.

By then a route had been selected for the first transcontinental railroad. It followed the old Overland Trail most of the way. The government had agreed to loan two separate companies $48,000 per mile for the construction of this road. The Central Pacific Company was to start clearing land for the right-of-way from Sacramento and work east. The Union Pacific Company was to start near what is now Omaha, Nebraska, and work west. There were no iron bridges at that time. Rivers and gorges had to be spanned by wooden structures before the tracks could be laid.

Building a railroad through mountainous country was a difficult task for the Central Pacific Company. Hardwood timber for railroad ties had to be carried from the slopes of the Sierras. Iron rails, spikes, and other supplies had to be shipped from the East by way of Cape Horn. Tunnels had to be dug through ice and snow near mountain peaks and through rocks. Drinking water for men and beasts had to be hauled across 50 to 60 miles of desert, and labor was scarce. Chinese coolies were imported to do much of the work. It is said that they were lowered from high cliffs in wicker baskets to drill holes in the rocks for blasting and that the death toll was high.

The Union Pacific also had its troubles. Hardwood timber for ties had to be cut in Indiana and Ohio, then shipped down the Missouri River on rafts. The scarcity of labor here was also a problem. There were not enough settlers for such a dangerous job, and many of them were against the railroad's crossing their land. They were afraid that sparks from the wood-burning engines would set fire to their homes, crops, and stores. The greatest trouble, however, was from hostile Indians, who constantly attacked the men while at work.

It took hundreds of men to clear a right-of-way in such hostile country, and they had to be fed. Buffalo were plentiful. Hunters were hired to supply the cooks with buffalo hindquarters. Thousands of these huge beasts were killed every week. Fur dealers in the East also were begging for buffalo hides to supply their customers. Greedy hunters even put guns in the hands of hostile Indians and told them to shoot and strip the animals of their hides.

By then the old flintlock rifles had been replaced by lightweight Smith and Wessons. The Indians loved these guns and would trade several of their best horses for one. Soon the prairies were strewn with the rotting carcasses of buffalo.

As the rails pushed farther and farther across the plains, the destruction of the buffalo increased until the

Indians became desperate. The once vast herds were fast disappearing, and the Indians suddenly realized that they could not survive without these marvelous animals. They relied upon them not only as a source of meat, but also for their hides, which provided a covering for their tepees and also clothing, bedding, war shields, leggings, moccasins, medicine pouches, and water bags. The horns provided cups, spoons, and bowls. Even the dung was used as fuel to feed their fires since there were no trees.

Oddly, there was no scurvy among the Plains Indians until after the buffalo were killed off. Buffalo meat evidently provided a full diet whether eaten fresh or sliced thin and dried (jerky) ready to eat or made into pemmican by grinding the meat and mixing it with equal parts of buffalo fat and dried wild berries. When molded into cakes and wrapped in green leaves, this mixture would last indefinitely.

Regardless of hostile or frightened Indians, the building of the railroad continued. In 1860, Congress appropriated money to stretch a telegraph wire across the country from coast to coast. This too was a dangerous task. Many of the poles had to be carried hundreds of miles by wagon across treeless plains and deserts. At first, the Indians were afraid of the "singing wire." They cut down the poles and carried away the wire until troops were sent out to protect the workers and the poles. Once started, the Western Union Telegraph crawled across the plains like a huge snake, following the railroad right-of-way most of the time.

By then the government was more determined than ever to move all the Indian tribes to reservations and teach them how to make a living at farming. The Indians did not want to live on a reservation, however. They wanted to live their own lives as they had always done, and those who were not already confined fought in every way they knew to protect their freedom.

7. The Civil War Period

THE THREAT OF a civil war over the right or wrong of slavery hung like a dark cloud over the entire nation. There was talk of the Southern states' seceding from the Union. The federal government had more pressing business than Indian wars.

New Mexico Territory was deeply concerned, however. Sentiment there was slightly on the side of the proslavery states. Most wealthy Mexicans and a few Anglo-Americans owned slaves. It was estimated that between 500 and 600 Navajo women and children were being held as slaves in wealthy homes. A doctor who had the opportunity to observe the situation and whose word was unimpeachable testified, "The trade in Navajo slaves is as regular as the trade in sheep or goats."

It was a toss-up which way the territory would go if war was declared. Regardless of how it went, the Indian agent Lieutenant Christopher (Kit) Carson pointed out to those in the Santa Fe and Taos areas that their main problem was still an Indian problem, and Kit should have known.

Former trapper, trader, and Indian fighter, Kit Carson knew the Indians far better than most white men knew them. He had been appointed lieutenant of rifles, United States Army, by President Polk for his services in 1847. He had also served successfully as agent to the Utes since 1853 and well knew that the Indian problem could not be solved by sending out small groups of green recruits to fight skilled warriors like the Navajo.

Unaware that trouble was brewing between the states, the Navajo knew only that officers and foot soldiers were leaving Fort Defiance. Believing this to be a sign of weakness, several leaders considered it a good time to attack the fort and run the Anglo-Americans out of their country. Resentment against the military had been building since Major Brooks had stolen their grazing ground and killed their stock. This resentment was deepened by white traders who exchanged bad whiskey and inferior guns for fine horses.

Manuelito and Barboncito were in favor of an attack. "The Anglo soldiers and officers are running away," Barboncito insisted. "We are stronger than the Anglos. Now is the time for us to strike." Ganado Mucho, the peacemaker, was against it. However, most of the chiefs at the council agreed, and messengers were sent out into neighboring Indian country to invite the Utes, Apaches, and Pueblo to join them in war.

In March 1860 some 2,000 warriors, mostly Navajo, armed with bows, arrows, lances, and a few guns, entered the Bonito Hills to attack the fort. At the head of the war party, the Navajo leaders riding spirited horses presented a terrifying aspect. They wore caps made from the heads of wildcats, mountain lions, skunk, and badgers with an eagle feather at the top. They carried shields made of several thicknesses of buckskin and were armed with bows and poisoned arrows. Although most of the warriors were on foot, their long lances (with sharp, poisoned tips) made

Barboncito, Navajo chief, photographed before 1870. Courtesy Smithsonian Institution National Anthropological Archives.

them look formidable, and some of them carried clubs with stone heads. Only a few had guns.

The officers at the fort were prepared, having been warned of the attack by Ute scouts. Artillery had been placed in several strategic spots. When the warriors were well within the compound, cannons exploded and guns boomed. Caught offguard and trapped between the walls of the Bonito Hills, the Indians fought a bloody two-hour battle. By then so many of them lay dead or wounded that all the remaining few could do was turn and run.

Even though the troops had won the battle against the Navajo, the morale of the soldiers was low. So many officers and foot soldiers had deserted to join the Federals or Confederates that the remaining troops were discouraged. Had it not been for their respect for, and trust in, their leader, the slight five-foot-six, gray-eyed frontiersman, Kit Carson, they would not have held together. His frontier exploits had already made him a national hero. The soldiers, Mexican or Anglo-American, believed what he said. But there were not enough troops left in the territory to protect the settlements or the relay stations. Moreover, since the mailcoaches had been discontinued, after two bridges between Missouri and the Rockies were burned down, with war imminent, the need to keep a line of communication open between the East and the West was more important than ever.

To remedy this situation, three men, Russell, Majors, and Waddell, formed a company to transport important mail across the country by horseback. This company was called The Pony Express. The owners ran an advertisement in a local newspaper that read; "Wanted. Young riders, quick, responsive and wiry. Not over 18 years of age. Orphans preferred. Wages $25.00 a month."

There were many answers to this ad. By April 1860,

relay stations were established every 20 to 25 miles with fresh mounts waiting for the youthful riders who streaked across the 2,000 miles of Indian country between St. Joseph, Missouri, and Sacramento, California, carrying mail pouches that weighed less than 20 pounds each.

By then so many soldiers had deserted Fort Defiance that it was abandoned in 1861. Such were the conditions in New Mexico when Abraham Lincoln was inaugurated president of the United States in 1861. By then six Southern states had seceded from the Union and elected Jefferson Davis as their president. When President Lincoln called for volunteers, Kit Carson resigned as Indian agent to accept the appointment of lieutenant colonel of the First Regiment of New Mexican volunteers.

In May 1861, William T. Sherman also offered his services to the federal government and accepted the appointment of brigadier general, commander of the regular New Mexican forces. During his short span of civilian life, he had been instrumental in pushing the Union Pacific Railroad forward. He never doubted the outcome or the effect a transcontinental railroad would have in unifying the nation.

The telegraph line, completed at Salt Lake City, Utah, in October, carried as its first message: "THE WEST IS LOYAL TO THE UNION." Nevertheless, the Civil War did not affect the Southwest as much as it did other parts of the country. New Mexico was invaded by Confederate soldiers, and some buildings were destroyed. The Confederates were quickly defeated by Union soldiers and forced to leave the country.

The tragic mistakes that followed in the handling of Indian affairs cannot be blamed altogether on corrupt or inefficient officials. A few were honest and did what they could, under the circumstances, to help the Indians. Their efforts were hampered by lack of adequate communication between the red men and the whites, by racial prejudice, and by the uncertain legal status of the Indians. Owing to the illegibility of the land grants handed out by both the Spanish and Mexican governments, it was assumed by the military government that when the United States purchased New Mexico Territory, the land became public domain and the Indians had no legal rights. This left them without either the advantage of citizenship or the right to occupy the land they had lived on for hundreds of years.

Most of those in authority agreed with Sherman that the Indians should be sent to reservations as far from civilization as possible.

In September 1862, during the midst of the Civil War, Congress passed the Homestead Act, which allowed settlers to acquire title to as many as 160 acres of land simply by living on the land for five years, improving it, and paying a fee of $10. With the passage of this act, thousands of land-hungry Easterners pulled up stakes and followed the advice of the journalist and political leader Horace Greeley to "Go West." But no one explained this act to the Indians or prepared them for the invasion that followed.

General James Carleton, commander of the New Mexican volunteers, had his own idea of how to control the Indians, especially the Navajo. His main idea was to exterminate the whole tribe on the theory that it was cheaper to kill them than to feed them, but this, of course, was not allowed. By November of 1862, he ordered a board of four officers to convene at the Bosque Redondo Valley on the Pecos River and select a site for a post to be named Fort Sumner. After inspecting the treeless valley that lay in the curve of the river, 14 miles from a clump of cottonwood trees from which it derived its name, they turned in their report to the general. The report said, in effect, that there was no pasture for the regimental mounts; the water was so alkaline it was not fit to drink; there was no wood for building or cooking; the river overflowed each spring; and the nearest supply depot was a long distance away.

Regardless of the board's disapproval, General Carleton had made up his mind. Fort Sumner and a reservation would be built at the Bosque. As far as he was concerned, it was ideally located for the confinement of troublesome Indian tribes, such as the Navajo and the Apache. With the river as its western boundary and barren land stretching eastward for hundreds of miles to the Staked Plains, it would stand as a barrier to the marauding Comanches and Kiowas, who had long used the valley as a rendezvous for invading New Mexico Territory. It also would block the Navajo and Apache from their devastating raids south of the border.

There were other reasons for moving these tribes so far away, however. The land they now occupied contained some of the richest mineral and grazing lands in the territory. By removing them to the Bosque, the government could control the mineral rights, which would be of value to the territory. Those in control of such matters agreed with General Carleton, and the work of building Fort Sumner began.

General Carleton's first move was to have the Mescalero Apaches, a small tribe, rounded up and sent to the reservation—not too difficult a task. He then would raid the Navajo, but first he had to establish a post large enough to hold them until the whole tribe could be rounded up. Again he authorized a board of officers to inspect a site near the head spring of the Ojo del Galla River in a valley that spread out in two directions, one leading to Zuñi, the other to Acona and Luguna. His predecessor had selected this site for a fort a year ago and had reported that there was plenty of timber for building and also a large plot of flat land for pasture, parade grounds, officers' quarters, barracks, and storerooms.

Following this investigation, the board of officers reported favorably, and work was begun immediately on Fort Canby. After visiting the site and surrounding country, General Carleton realized it would be necessary to build still another fort near the Canyon de Chelly, the Navajo stronghold.

Again a board of officers was sent out to inspect the area. This time they decided that Fort Defiance, even though it had deteriorated and was badly in need of repairs, was the most logical site for a fort in that area.

Carelton was pleased with this report. He would have the buildings repaired and the grounds cleared. In the meantime, he sent word to several Navajo chieftains, whose bands had been accused of driving off large flocks of sheep from the Isoleto, San Felipe, and Albuquerque districts, that he had an important offer to make them.

The Navajo did not know what to think of the constantly shifting policies of the white men or of the constant changing of the military men who attempted to control them or of the Indian agents who were sent out with each successive administration in Washington. They had learned not to trust the white men, yet several chieftains arrived for the council carrying long lances 3 to 6 feet long, the handles decorated with eagle feathers.

General Carleton made them welcome and the meeting seemed to be going well until he informed them that the Great White Father in Washington had instructed him to offer them a large tract of land far away from towns or settlements where they could raise their children and tend their flocks in peace. He also assured them that there would be ample pasture and water for their flocks, plenty of land for their crops, a blacksmith shop and a cemetery where they could bury their dead.

Barboncito was a shrewd man. He stood looking at Carleton a moment before asking where was this land the Great White Father wanted to give them.

When General Carleton told him that it was at the Bosque Redondo on the Pecos River, Barboncito shook his head. He had heard about this land from a Mescalero Apache, who had managed to slip away from the reservation, and knew that it was worthless. His dark eyes filled with anger when he informed the General that his people would not agree to go there—that the Navajo were a powerful nation and that they would stay in their own country.

This, in turn, made the General very angry and he replied in no uncertain terms that the Great White Father had lost faith in the Navajo, that their word was no good and for them to go home and tell their people that if they did not go peacefully to the Bosque Redondo, they would be forced to go there.

The headmen sat in silence for some time, pondering the situation. When they did not speak, Carleton again reminded them that they had no choice. They either would go peacefully to this far away reservation, or the men would be killed, the women and children taken prisoners, and their crops destroyed.

A few of the "enemy Navajo" from the Mt. Taylor region under Sandoval agreed to go. The other headmen got to their feet and without speaking filed out of the meeting in silence.

General Carleton was disappointed—this meant war. Maybe it was just as well. This would give him an opportunity to kill off all those who refused to surrender, and he

Manuelito, noted Navajo war chief of 1855–1872, photographed by Ben Wittick during a visit to Washington, D.C., in 1874. He died during the winter of 1893. Courtesy Smithsonian Institution National Anthropological Archives, Bureau of American Ethnology Collection.

knew who could take charge of such a campaign. He and Colonel Christopher Carson had long been friends. Kit would find a way to conquer them—force them into submission or death.

Even though they would not admit it, the Navajo were frightened. Their neighbors, the Mascalero Apaches, were the first Indians in the Southwest to be sent to a reservation. They could not understand why they had to give up their country to the land-hungry Anglo-Americans. Neither did they understand why they did not have the same right to kill and rob these invaders as the Anglo-Americans. If this meant an all-out war, they would fight, even though they had only a few guns and a small amount of ammunition.

8. Destroy and Conquer

In April 1863, General Carleton ordered Kit Carson to make his headquarters at Fort Canby and from there plan a campaign against the Navajo in the Chaco Mountain area. His orders were to first send out word for them to surrender or be killed.

If this ultimatum did not bring them in, Carson was ordered to kill the men who refused to surrender, capture the women, children, and stock; destroy the crops, fences, orchards, and burn the hogans. The sheep and goats that could not be used as food for soldiers were to be killed.

He also was instructed to promise the prisoners food and clothing and hospitals for the sick and aging, if they would go peacefully to the Bosque Redondo, and to hold them at the Fort until they could be moved.

Kit Carson did not like this assignment. His sympathies were with the Navajo. His first wife had been an Arapahoe and the mother of his beloved daughter, Adelaide. He knew of many instances when the Navajo had been blamed for depredations committed by other tribes. He had just finished rounding up the Mescalero Apaches and moving them to the barren plains of the Bosque Redondo after they had been promised a "Garden of Eden."

He had no desire to destroy the haughty Navajo, but the general wanted a large showing of captured Indians to justify the building of Fort Sumner. All Carson could do was to execute the order, and he would do it to the best of his ability.

The Navajo were a large tribe, however. If the leaders ever once got together and organized a war, they would be far stronger than his own small army. This did not particularly worry him. Navajo chieftains had never been known to agree on a war. Had they agreed, they would have won the battle at Fort Defiance. There was little danger of their getting together now. Owing to the ruggedness of the mountainous country they occupied, all they had to do was to hide in the canyons until the danger was over; and he well knew his campaign could fail unless he had Utes for guides and trackers. The Utes were almost as familiar with Navajo country as they were their own. Moreover, since he had been their agent, he felt confident they not only would obey him, but would also be loyal.

In a message to General Carleton, he asked permission to employ 100 Ute warriors to act as trackers and guides. The Utes were not afraid of the Navajo and were brave and fine shots. Because of these qualities, Carson felt that one hundred Ute warriors would be of more service to him in rounding up the Navajo than twice their number in untrained soldiers.

The request was granted.

With an army of 20 officers; a few regular soldiers; and some 400 volunteers, who needed the extra money they could make soldiering, Colonel Carson took up his headquarters at Fort Wingate and sent out word for the Navajo leaders to come to the fort for a talk.

When they arrived in July 1863, the Rope Thrower, as the Indians called Carson, explained why it was necessary for them to surrender and encourage their tribesmen to give themselves up. "The Father in Washington is tired of your broken promises and crooked talk," he told them. "He intends to stop your raiding and fighting. If you do not surrender and go peacefully to the reservation they have set aside for you, I have been ordered to hunt you down and kill you regardless of how long it takes."

"But if you will surrender and go peacefully, you and your families will be clothed, fed, and housed until you can plant your crops and raise your sheep, so that your women can weave their rugs and blankets without fear of being captured or sold as slaves. You have until July 20 to gather up your flocks and come to the fort. After that date you will be considered hostile and hunted down like wolves."

A few of the Mt. Taylor chieftains in the group agreed to go to the reservation with their families. Others, who lived back in the mountains and who had never warred against the Mexicans, Americans, or signed a treaty, stood off to one side. "We refuse to leave our mountains," they told him. "We are as powerful as you. If you come to take us, we will kill you."

Colonel Carson began his campaign in late July. Before his troops started out, however, they were given a small amount of salt, sugar, flour, and coffee. There was no need to burden them with extra food. The Navajos' fields were filled with ripening grains, beans, squash, sweet potatoes, and melons at this time of year; and the orchards were ripe with fruit. After satisfying their hunger, the troops were ordered to destroy all of the Navajos' crops, gardens, and orchards and to burn all the hogans. They also were told to kill all the livestock they could not capture or drive back to the fort.

The colonel's volunteer army was a motley-looking crew. A few of them wore hand-me-down uniforms. Most

Colonel Christopher (Kit) Carson, photographed in the early 1860s. Courtesy of the Kit Carson Memorial Foundation, Inc., Taos, N.M.

of the uniforms, however, were handmade of material their wives had patched together. The Ute trackers and guides wore breechcloths. Only the officers were mounted.

Since the volunteers did not have mounts, the colonel divided the men into small units, each with a Ute guide. They were instructed to spread out over the country and cover as much ground as possible. They were also to lie in wait at water holes for Indians to appear or track them to their hideouts.

It was a difficult campaign. The hot, midsummer sun poured down without mercy, especially after a sudden rainstorm that soaked their clothing and backpacks; and at night they often had to march over land pitted with prairie dog holes to find water. Despite all the planning, tracking, and scouting, the soldiers went for days without seeing a Navajo man, woman, or child. "Some of them escaped into Hopi country," Carson's men were told by the villagers. Others had gone as far west as the Grand Canyon to join tribes there. Still others had crossed the border into Mexico. What few were left in that part of the country had simply disappeared into the maze of small canyons and crevices. Only a few were captured or surrendered.

This was a frustrating situation for an Indian fighter and frontiersman such as Colonel Carson. Discouraged by such poor results, he promised his men, with the general's permission, a bounty of $20 a head for all sound, service-able horses or mules delivered to the fort, and a dollar a head for all sheep or goats.

This generosity did not produce the desired results. Only a few sheep, goats, horses, or mules were turned in at the fort, and even fewer Navajo captives. In a desperate effort to round up more Navajo, the colonel took it upon himself to offer his men the privilege of selling the women or children they captured to wealthy Mexican families as house slaves. They would be better cared for than if sent to the Bosque, where they would be a burden on the government. He felt the same way about adult captives. If they could be distributed among Mexican families, it would save the government, already up to its neck in a civil war, a tremendous expense; and the Navajo would be better off than crowded on the dry, treeless plains of the Bosque Redondo.

General Carleton did not agree with the colonel. When he learned of Kit's plans to dispose of the captured women and children, he ordered all captives, regardless of age or sex, to be delivered to the fort without exception.

By mid-October a delegation of Navajo chieftains from the Chaco Mountain area arrived at the fort to sue for peace, but it was too late. They were told in no uncertain terms that they had been given ample warning—that they must now surrender and go to the reservation or be hunted down, one at a time if necessary, until all were captured or killed. Colonel Carson also reminded them that winter was just ahead and that it would not take long for them to consume the food, water, and wood they had stored for winter use. On the other hand, if they surrendered, they would be fed, clothed, and allowed to retain their flocks of sheep. They were then told to return to their people and advise them to give themselves up.

Ganado Mucho ("Long Earrings") and other chieftains urged their people to surrender. "If we keep fighting, we will soon be dragged down the white man's road and only coyotes will live on our land. If we surrender and go in peace, we may be allowed to return to our land some day."

These words were lost against the words of Barboncito, Manuelito, and other hostile chiefs. Moreover, even though their crops were destroyed, their orchards chopped down, and their sheep killed, only 108 Navajo families showed up at Fort Wingate.

On January 6, 1864, Colonel Carson received word to move his headquarters to Fort Defiance and plan a campaign against the Navajo in the Canyon de Chelly region. The weather was intensely cold in northern Arizona by then, but Carson's ragged army made it to the fort without mishap.

Snow already was two inches deep in places. A winter campaign called for a great deal of planning. Carson had no more than settled down for this purpose when the roll of Indian war drums could be heard reverberating from one canyon wall to another in the distance, warning the Navajo of impending war.

In the past, neither Mexican nor American troops had succeeded in campaigning against the Navajo in this region or in penetrating their mighty stronghold, the Canyon de Chelly. "But there must be some way to conquer it," the colonel mused.

9. Invasion of Canyon de Chelly

DURING THE WORST snowstorm of the season, Colonel Kit Carson left Fort Defiance with 20 mounted officers, some 400 volunteers on foot, and several army wagons loaded with artillery and supplies. The march against the traditionally impregnable Canyon de Chelly, some 20 miles north, was on its way. It was almost impossible, though, for the men on foot, the horses, or the oxen to travel through such deep snow.

Carson had asked General Carleton for more horses or mules for his men, but the general had replied, "The time to strike is now while the snow is deep and the Indians are holed up in caves. The men must travel light and expect to suffer some discomfort or the war will be lost. However, I am sending you 38 mules. I hope there will be no more reports of army mules' being stolen."

The snow was deep, so deep that a detachment of men had to be sent ahead with picks and shovels to break a trail for the rest of the men and the wagons to follow. They covered only five miles that first day. When evening came, the weary soldiers were more than ready to bed down.

Bedding down in six to twelve inches of snow was not

a simple task in the Rockies. The officers carried a couple of woolen blankets under their saddles. Those on foot carried the blankets in their backpacks. The problem was to keep one blanket dry for the next night out. To do this two men generally slept together. A horse blanket was spread on the ground or rocky cove, and two blankets spread over it. The great coats the men wore were then spread over the blankets. It is claimed the men slept comfortably warm between the tightly woven wool blankets and that each had a dry blanket for the next night.

The second day out, Colonel Carson ordered Captain Pfeiffer with a detachment of 100 men and supplies to march to the eastern entrance of the Canyon de Chelly—the del Muerto entrance—the "Canyon of the Dead." They were to make camp there, guard the entrance, and meet him in the canyon in two days.

When the captain and his men were on their way, Carson and his troops forged on toward the western entrance. The Chinle, it was called, meaning the "Coming-out Place." It took five days for them to reach their destination. Several oxen died of exhaustion along the way. Two men's feet were frozen, and several supply wagons had to be left along the trail.

When finally they reached the Chinle and were about to bed down for the night, several Navajo braves came to the camp under a flag of truce, wanting to surrender. After they had been fed, they were told to return to their hogans, round up their stock and appear at Fort Defiance with their families within ten days.

The next morning several more Navajo came to the camp and told the colonel they would have surrendered before had they not been warned by traders that this was a war of extermination. They too were fed, given warm blankets, and advised to surrender at the fort with their stock and families within ten days.

Before Colonel Carson began his tour of destruction, he picked several of his best trackers to scout the northern rim of the canyon for trails or tracks leading to the bottom of the gorge and several more to scout the southern rim. At the last moment he decided to accompany the men scouting the southern rim.

This was the first time the famous frontiersman had been near the mouth of this mighty canyon, and he, like all the others, stood in silence as he gazed down into its awesome depths. Then he stood gazing at the cliff dwellings that dotted the higher ledges. He had heard the legend of the "Gone away People," whose spirits still guarded the Navajo, and he could not keep from wondering just what he was getting into. Some of the finest soldiers of the Southwest had waged war against the Navajo in this mighty fortress and failed. Just how far would he and his men get before they were picked off, he wondered.

The next day (January 18, 1864), Colonel Carson and his soldiers made their way through the snow down a faint trail leading to the bottom of the gorge. He cautioned his men to keep close together and be prepared to defend themselves if necessary. As they entered the yawning mouth of the canyon, they were met by a small band of hostile warriors, who were quickly conquered and sent to the fort under guard. Carson was surprised, though, by the lack of resistance. He had no way of knowing that the Navajo leaders, when they saw the strength of the army and the artillery, had advised their people to hide until the danger was over.

The troops could see men, women, and children hovering on high ledges in the cold and could hear the curses and taunts hurled down at them, but they made no move to retaliate. The general's plan was to starve them into submission, and that was just what Carson intended to do.

The stream that flowed through the valley was covered with ice, but there was very little snow. And back in the sheltered coves where the chasm widened were orchards and fields of standing corn that looked as if they had not been touched by frost.

By then the Navajo had eaten most of the food they had stored and had used up their drinking water. When the war drums had warned them to take cover, they had gathered as much corn as possible, but not all. Now, as the soldiers went along burning and chopping down their fields of ripened corn and their precious peach trees whose roots stemmed from saplings the Spanish fathers had given the Hopi, they trembled in fear and sorrow. Each blow, echoing down the canyon, told them their way of life was coming to an end. The soldiers were not content just to chop down the trees; they burned the branches and the stumps, so that the people could not even suck a little nourishment from the bark.

The Navajo were not given to self-pity; but when the soldiers slaughtered their flocks of sheep and goats, dumped them in piles, and burned the carcasses, it was more than even they could endure. The Navajo did not take it in silence. They rolled huge boulders off high ledges down on the destroyers, but it did not stop the slaughter. It is said that so many sheep and goats were killed during that raid that the stench of the rotting bones lasted for years.

As the soldiers continued to move from field to field, from orchard to orchard, from flock to flock, the Navajo realized they had no intention of leaving until every living thing was destroyed.

When it rained one night, several Navajo women and children caught rain water and gathered enough brush, while the soldiers were asleep, for a small fire and enough bones from a pile of slaughtered sheep to make a pot of soup. But after the soup was made, as hungry as they were, they could not eat it.

The more Carson's campaign succeeded, the more depressed he became. His dreams were haunted by starving Navajo, especially women and children; but this did not keep him from finishing what he had started. By then Captain Pfeiffer and his men, with 90 prisoners, had joined the colonel and his troops.

The task of laying waste the impregnable canyon was completed by the end of the sixth day. And as far as Carson could see, it was the home of only a small portion of the Navajo tribe. There was not enough grass or plots of land on the floor of the Canyon de Chelly to support more than a few thousand people at one time.

By then word had been passed that the "Rope Thrower" was not killing his captives. One evening over a hundred men, women and children came to his camp to surrender. Later three women appeared with a white cloth tied to a stick and demanded to know why his troops were destroying their crops and capturing their sheep.

Through an interperter, Carson attempted to explain that they had to leave their old home where they had caused so much trouble and move to a reservation where they could be clothed and fed until they could make a living for themselves, and where they could live in peace and weave their rugs without fear of being captured or sold as slaves.

He then warned them that if they did not surrender and go peacefully, they would be hunted down like wolves, regardless of how long it took to finish the job. He then advised them to go back and tell their people to surrender before it was too late.

Colonel Carson was as anxious to return to the fort as his men. He wanted to be there when the starving, ragged Navajo began to arrive. Over 200 men, women, and children followed the troops back to the fort, and several were there waiting for him. A few of the Navajo rode horses; others drove in a few sheep they had managed to hide; but the majority were without livestock, food, or clothing.

Forced through hunger into submission, they had left their canyons, their blue sky stones and their gods and had submitted to the white man's will; but they did it with a lump in their throats and dry, unblinking eyes.

By the first of February, 1864, nearly 1,000 more Navajo had come to the fort to await transfer to the Bosque Redondo. By the middle of February, several hundred more appeared. The soldiers handed out what blankets and army tents they could spare, but there were not enough to go around. Some of the Navajo threw together makeshift hogans of brush and logs; others huddled around small fires to keep warm.

White flour, beans, bacon, and green coffee were given to them, as well as a few cooking utensils; but the Navajo did not know how to prepare such strange food or use the cook pans.

On March 6, 1864, a long train of army wagons filled with supplies lined up at Fort Defiance to escort the captives to their new home. Over 2,500 Navajo left the fort that day to begin the long, painful 400-mile walk to the Bosque Redondo. A command of soldiers rode at the head of the long procession, and one at the rear. The weather was still miserably cold. Snow drifting across the trail made traveling difficult. Only the very old and the very young were allowed to ride on the wagons. A few of the men rode horses and carried a child or two behind them. Most of the children had to walk or be carried by their mothers.

With the soldiers behind them, they had to keep going, and as the frightened, weary people trudged along, many of the older men and women, who no longer could keep up the pace, crawled off to one side of the trail and died. The Navajo, even though they were afraid of death, would have buried their dead had they been allowed; but the train of wagons did not stop. The People had to keep moving at the rate of ten to twelve miles a day. The trail of the long walk from Fort Defiance to Fort Wingate was marked by frozen bodies.

Some historians tell us that Kit Carson rode along beside the marchers that first day with a weary child or two on the saddle with him. Full of pity for the proud race, he gave them what encouragement he could, but encouragement was not what they needed. They needed time to rest their weary bodies and sore feet.

The trail lay south and east. At night the captives were hearded into a large circle surrounded by the supply wagons. Fires were built for warmth and for cooking the meager supply of food. Soldiers went among them, showing the women how to mix the flour with water, pat it into flat cakes, and wrap it around a stick and cook it over a bed of coals. The women also were taught how to grind the green coffee beans into a coarse meal before boiling them.

Each day more and more ragged, hungry Navajo who had been hiding in the canyons joined the line of march. Several hundred were picked up at Fort Canby. The walk from Fort Defiance to Fort Wingate was one of horror. Slave raiders, enemy Utes, and drifters lay in wait to prey on each group as it passed. Several young mothers were captured and thrown across a horse, the baby in their arms thrown to the ground or tossed over a cliff.

Over a thousand Navajo were waiting at Fort Wingate to join the others on their way to Fort Sumner. By now it seemed that a good portion of the tribe was on the move. Food became scarce. Young braves were sent out with soldiers to hunt deer, buffalo, and small game. Game was scarce, however. Many nights the captives went to bed hungry.

When finally the marchers reached the village of Los Pinos on the Rio Grande, they stopped for supplies and for the captain in charge of the train to find the best place to cross. Spring rains flooded the Rio, making it dangerous.

The thought of crossing the river terrified the Navajo. They had never been near so large a body of water and did not know how to swim. The women with babies were piled into wagons and taken across. The others had to get over the best way they knew how. Many of them clung frantically to wagon tailgates, the tails of horses, sheep, or goats. When the sheep and the goats were swept downstream by the strong current, so were hundreds of Navajo.

On the eastern bank, fires were built to warm the half-drowned people. They were given time to dry their clothes and count the members of their families. Only a few of those washed downstream managed to drag themselves back to the crossing. The loss of members of their families created panic and despair.

The medicine men went among them and did what they could. "This is a dark night for the Diné," the medicine men intoned gravely. "We have been forced to leave our homes and our gods, but the time will come when we will return. Have courage."

Two days later, the wagon train again headed southeast for Fort Sumner and the Bosque Redondo. By now the country had changed. The air grew warmer; and as they passed great stretches of grape vines and apricot orchards, watered by irrigation ditches, they marveled at what they saw. But as they continued to travel east, they left the beautiful valley of the Rio Grande behind and entered a flat, desolate, treeless land covered with strange-looking grass and throny bushes that tumbled across the plains in the wind.

It took them nearly 12 weeks to reach their destination. The tragic, heartbreaking journey was over, but not their unshed tears.

10. The Bosque Redondo

By THE MIDDLE of May, over 7,000 destitute Navajo men, women, and children were encamped at Fort Sumner on the mesquite-covered plains of the Bosque Redondo. As they passed through the gates of the fort, they were counted and given ration tickets. Then they stood gazing at the "Garden of Eden" they had been promised. They viewed the flat, barren plains with dismay.

With all his planning, General Carleton had been so harassed by the citizens to "get the Navajo out of the country" that he had not prepared for so many captives. The fort was still under construction. The officers' quarters, barracks, bakery, commissary, warehouse, and hospital for the soldiers had been erected; and the corrals, fenced. But no preparation had been made to shelter the Navajo! Nor had enough food, seeds, or farm tools been procured to feed them or plant their crops.

Suddenly conscious that the growing season already was far advanced and that the Navajo were supposed to be self-supporting, the general frantically sent a request to Lorenzo Thomas, adjutant general of the army, for 2,000,000 pounds of foodstuffs to be sent in installments of 500,000 pounds each. Carleton also wanted blankets, farm tools, axes, spades, knives, plows, and various kinds of seeds. He told Thomas, "The surrendered Navajo are at our mercy and must be given food and clothing until their crops mature. I respectfully urge you to send the necessary supplies to the fort as soon as possible."

The general then sent a message to the fort commander, Major Henry Wallen, to procure all the Navajos' sheep and goats that were not fit for breeding and to slaughter them for food.

The Navajo, hungry for cornmeal, accepted the white flour and slabs of bacon handed out to them, but those who had not learned how to bake the flour into cakes ate the dough raw or in a thin gruel. Moreover, most of them did not know what to do with the slabs of bacon that had been left on shelves so long that they had spoiled. Over a hundred of the captives died of dysentery during the first few weeks.

When a month passed and the promised rations, seeds, and farm tools had not arrived, the general again sent a frantic message to the adjutant general, then instructed Major Wallen to ration all the food at the fort, including that for the soldiers until more could be procured.

The first installment of food, when it did arrive, was anything but adequate. After being transported by oxen in warm weather from Fort Leavenworth, Kansas, to the reservation, the flour and cornmeal were infested with weevil; and the beef, shipped in barrels, had spoiled.

Somehow the majority of the Navajo managed to survive. Those who were not ill or too old to work were put to clearing a 3,000-acre plot covered with thorny grass and mesquite bushes. This had to be done before the land could be plowed. The roots of the mesquite were tough and went deep into the earth and had to be grubbed out.

Fort Sumner, New Mexico. Old post on the Pecos River.
Courtesy of General Services Administration, National
Archives and Records Service, Washington, D.C. (U.S.
Siganl Corps photo no. 111-SC-87974)

Since there were not enough digging tools to go around, the women and children had to dig up the roots with their bare hands or sharp rocks.

When finally the land was cleared and plowed, each family was allotted 20 acres to plant in corn, beans, squash, melons, and pumpkins. The land was so dry that water had to be carried by hand from the river and poured over the seeds before they could sprout.

The Navajo did not like the white man's way of farming. Most of them were accustomed to planting their crops with a sharp, pointed stick or the shoulder bone of a deer. Only a few from the Canyon de Chelly region knew how to handle a hoe, spade, or a one-man plow. Nor did they like the Mexican soldiers standing over them, telling them what to do and seeing that they kept busy. Always before, when planting their fields, they could stop and rest when they grew tired. Now they were forced to keep going no matter how they felt. This, of course, created resentment.

The general as well as other officials of Indian affairs still could not seem to understand that no race or ethnic group could be easily forced into changing its way of life in a short time. Had there been any clear communication between those in charge and the Navajo, conditions and personal feelings might have been different. But there was no one at the Bosque to interpret for them other than a fourteen-year-old Mexican youth, Juan Arviso, called Soos, who had been brought up by the Navajo. He could speak only a few words of Spanish.

By then most of the Navajo chiefs who had refused to surrender were forced through hunger to join their tribes at the Bosque. Manuelito, in buckskins with a blanket thrown over his shoulder, and carrying a lance, arrived with some of his band. Later, Barboncito arrived with some of his group and also Delgadito, a Ute who lived with the Navajo.

There was a drought that summer. Ditches had to be dug by hand so that the brackish water of the Pecos could reach the struggling plants. The beans had just started to bloom and the corn to tassel when great swarms of grasshoppers settled on the plants and stripped them of their leaves.

As the days passed, the hungry, unhappy Navajo grew more and more homesick for their beloved mountains. Each time an allotment of food arrived, the flour was contaminated, and the beef was always spoiled. This kind of treatment did not set well with them. The "Garden of Eden" had turned out to be a place of misery, hunger, and despair.

Some of the warriors made arrows from pieces of scrap iron and broken bottles they had picked up around the fort. With these arrows, they hunted prairie dogs for food. Others, tired of the dreary life, slipped away from the reservation during the night in an effort to find food and some way to escape. They returned, however. They could not survive on the barren plains without water, and they did not know where to look for it in the dark.

Beyond the reservation there were no villages for over a hundred miles other than those of the Comanche, who had owned this land before white men had taken it for their own. The many enemies, as the Navajo called the Comanche, were skilled raiders who had not yet been converted to the white man's way of thinking. They often slipped onto the reservation at night and carried off the Navajos' horses, sheep, and goats and sometimes a woman. The Navajo had no way to fight back other than with bows and arrows, which were not always usable. On the reservation it was difficult for them to find suitable wood for bows and new sinew for strings.

Winter came early that year, and since no shelters had

been provided to protect them from the rain, snow, or cold wind that swept across the country from the Staked Plains—no blankets to keep them warm or sheep to shear for wool to weave into warm clothing—they had to dig holes in the ground. For a roof to cover the holes, they used anything they could find, from pieces of discarded tents to tin scraps or animal hides. They dared not use the mesquite bushes they had bunched in great piles. The bushes were the only fuel they had to burn for warmth and cooking.

General Carleton authorized spare army tents to be set up and empty grain sacks issued in an effort to help keep the Navajo warm, but they were not enough. When the cold wind piled snow a foot deep about the base of the damp, drafty holes, many of the very old and the very young died. It is said the holes made for those crude dwellings still show on the plain where the Bosque Redondo reservation once stood.

By midwinter the snow was so deep that ox-drawn freight trains could not travel the Santa Fe Trail. When the allotment of foodstuffs began to run low, rationing began again. Word leaked out that the Navajo were dying of starvation and exposure, and General Carleton feared that Congress would hear of it and return the Navajo to their own land. Such a move would defeat his purpose in sending them to the Bosque in the first place.

He would not admit, even to himself, that his Indian policy was an ill-planned failure. Instead, after much communication with the Indian agent at Washington, Congress finally agreed to pass a bill appropriating $100,000 to be used mainly for building 12 villages on the reservation and for setting up 12 courts, with a Navajo leader at the head of each.

The money for this project was entrusted to two men

who were to purchase the necessary supplies at Independence, Missouri, and deliver them to the reservation. Less than one third of this money ever reached its destination, not nearly enough to build the villages as planned.

By then it was spring. Time for the Navajo to start planting a new crop.

The summer of 1865 turned out to be almost as heartbreaking as the summer of 1864. In spite of the Navajos' hard work, cutworms, hailstones, and alkaline soil contributed to another crop failure, which meant that the government was again forced to issue thousands of dollars worth of rations.

The expense of caring for so many prisoners was costing the United States a great deal of money, and complaints were being made. Knowing this, a group of wealthy New Mexicans offered to relieve the government of part of its burden by "binding out" Navajo men and women to work in their homes and fields.

The offer was refused, but General Carleton knew he had to do something to stop the criticism. In an effort to furnish the prisoners with fresh meat, he ordered a thousand head of beef cattle on the hoof from Texas. Several hundred of them were stolen by hungry Indians along the trail. The cattle that survived such a long drive were nothing but skin and bones when they reached the reservation.

The general's next effort was to relieve Colonel Kit Carson of his duties at Fort Defiance so that he could supervise the building of the villages, which, for lack of funds, were to be constructed of logs and adobe bricks.

Neither Kit Carson nor the soldiers were skilled in building adobe dwellings, but they taught the Navajo how to make the bricks. In time, 12 villages of low, flat-topped, hutlike buildings were completed; and the Navajo moved in.

They had no more than settled, however, when a smallpox epidemic broke out. There were no doctors to minister to the sick or dying, and the medicine men, who still did not have even corn pollen or herbs to work with, could do little to help them.

Over 300 Navajo died within a few weeks that fall. The others, undernourished, ill-clothed, and disheartened, refused to live in dwellings where death had occurred. The spirit of a loved one was a very real thing to a Navajo. In the past, when a member of a family died, the hogan was burned; and a new one was built in a different location.

Knowing the Navajo and their traditional fears, Colonel Carson decided to leave space at the end of each row of dwellings open so that a new one could be built. In this way a family could move out of a dwelling where death had occurred into a new building. The old building could then be torn down and a new one erected. It was the only way he knew to solve the problem.

By now the civil authorities, as well as the military, were pointing to the general's mistakes and at Congress for appropriating $100,000 for a lost cause. In fact, the question of keeping the Navajo at the Bosque was becoming not only an issue in New Mexico's politics, but in Washington also. Now that the Civil War had ended, the East was becoming more and more interested in the West.

In April of 1865, William T. Sherman was commissioned lieutenant general of the military in the West and was pleased by the appointment. He was anxious to visit once again the vast expanse of land west of the Missouri River, which was still comparatively untouched. Its only drawback was its remoteness, and that would be remedied when the transcontinental railroad was completed. Fast and safe traveling between the East and the West would then be established, and perhaps peace would be restored.

During the fall of 1865, General Sherman studied the reports sent in from the Southwest to acquaint himself with current conditions. A report by Kit Carson was always interesting. Kit probably knew the West better than any other man alive, and what he had to say was important.

Among other things, Carson's report recommended that the control of Indian affairs be returned to the War Department. He also cited several instances of Indian chiefs in Kansas who complained that the bales of goods, sent to them by the Great White Father, shrank in size before they reached their destination. It seemed the agents took a little bit of the contents from each bale before sending it on to the next station, until the bales were so small when they reached the Indians that they were hardly worth receiving. Colonel Carson also pointed out that civil authorities were demanding more and more troops to protect the outposts. He reported that, every time an Indian party raided some isolated settlement, troops were ordered out to protect it. These authorities knew the Indians were finding it almost impossible to survive since their land had been gobbled up by these same settlers, and their main source of food, the buffalo, destroyed.

This information was distasteful to General Sherman. He wrote to his friend General Grant, general of all the armies of the United States: "The situation in the West will never be any better as long as the travelers insist on settling on Indian land and killing off, not only the buffalo, but men, women, and children and burning their villages."

In the spring of 1866, General Sherman began his tour of the Southwest. Before starting, however, he was asked by the quartermaster general to investigate the high cost of maintaining military posts on the Plains, especially in New Mexico. "See if expenses can be reduecd there," the message read.

Knowing how poor the United States Treasury was after fighting a costly war, General Sherman turned his attention on New Mexico.

"This is a large and thinly settled country," he wrote General Grant. "The people are a miserable lot of Mexicans, Indians, and a few whites who expect to make a fortune at military expense. The settlements in this part of the country have no market for their produce and the people are nuzzling at the government trough. The military out here pays all the expenses and do all the dirty work. General Carleton has not only retained his army of volunteers, he has increased the Third Cavalry to protect such settlements as Albuquerque and Santa Fe, who are well able to protect themselves. He also has rounded up some 7,000 Navajo and is holding them as prisoners of war on a miserable reservation below Fort Sumner. The Territory of New Mexico already has cost the government several million dollars, which will never contribute one red cent to the national income. I recommend that something be done about it."

Upon receipt of this information, General Grant sent General Carleton an order to muster out the volunteer army and bring the military down to its regular size. During this time, a new agent had been appointed to the Navajo and had brought with him 100 head of cattle and 17 wagons loaded with food, seeds, and farm implements. He then asked for a practical farm assistant to teach the Navajo a more modern way to farm.

In less than a month, however, he rescinded this order and recommended that no more money be spent on improving the Bosque Redondo. He also recommended that a committee be appointed to examine the Navajos' old territory and to select a site there where water, wood, and grazing land would be available as a permanent reservation.

By the spring of 1867, travel from the East to the West was on the increase, and Indians all over the country were becoming more and more hostile. The Department of the Interior was demanding greater control over the Indians, and the question of who should control the Bosque Redondo had again arisen in Washington. It was apparent to everyone familiar with Indian affairs in New Mexico that something had to be done about "Carleton's tragic mistake."

During the summer of 1867, through an act of Congress, the old Indian Peace Commission was reorganized. It was composed of General William T. Sherman, General William S. Harney, General Alfred H. Terry, and four civilians. A council was held at Fort Leavenworth, Kansas, August 13, to revolutionize the Indian Service as well as attempt to iron out many of the squabbles between the Indians and the whites.

The new commission bitterly criticized the Administration of Indian Affairs. It declared that the Indian tribes west of the Missouri River had cost the federal government over 30 million dollars and many lives and that still there was nothing but trouble. It recommended a complete revision of the intercourse laws pertaining to all the Indian tribes and suggested that Congress fix a date at which time all agents and special agents be relieved of their duty and replaced with more competent officials, men who had proved their worth.

It also asserted that all territorial governors and ex officio superintendents of Indian affairs or state legislatures should not be permitted to call out troops to wage war against the Indians. It did agree, however, on a policy to remove the warlike tribes from the neighborhood of railroads and to establish two great reservations, one to the north and one to the south, where the tribes would receive maintenance until they became self-supporting.

Finally, the commission asked that an agreement be made with the Navajo to remove them from the Bosque Redondo and to place them on a reservation in the South-west territory.

About this time, Theodore H. Dodd, former Indian agent, was appointed superintendent of Indian affairs. He proved to be a capable administrator and a friend to the Indians.

No doubt the civil government was eager to be rid of the Indian responsibility, but the transfer of the Navajo to the military did not take place until November 1, 1867.

11. The Treaty of Peace

SEVERAL MONTHS PASSED before the newly organized Peace Commission appointed a committee to investigate the disgraceful plight of the Navajo people at the Bosque Redondo. General Sherman was authorized to head this committee.

On May 28, 1868, the general with Colonel S. F. Tappan, also a member of the Peace Commission, and several other officers, arrived at Fort Sumner. The Peace Committee spent the next two days observing the diseased, half-naked, half-starved condition of the once proud Navajo, who had formerly owned over a quarter of a million sheep and some 60,000 horses.

"The government provided you with tools and seeds and you are experienced farmers. Why have you failed to make a crop these past four years?" General Sherman asked the group that stood near him.

Barboncito, who acted as spokesman through an interpreter, replied, "We have done our best. The white man's ways are not our ways. We pulled up mesquite roots and dug ditches, as ordered. But grasshoppers swarmed down and destroyed our crops the first year. Cutworms and drought destroyed them the second year. Hailstones and flood wiped them out the third year. We have given up."

Sherman, grim, tight-lipped, scowling, said with brutal frankness, "I believe what you have spoken. But why have you given up?"

"Because this land is worthless, and we are too weak to survive another year of hunger and hard work," Barboncito replied. "Nor can we fight off the Comanche, who steal our few sheep and carry off our women. We have no weapons."

The general looked thoughtful. "All people love the land where they were born, and the Comanche once owned this country. But this world is big enough for all the people to live together if they will live in peace and harmony. The Comanche and the Navajo are no more than seven leaves compared to all the leaves in the forest. If you agree, we will send you to a new reservation where there are trees, good water, and grazing for your sheep. And where you can live in peace with your neighbors."

"Where is this land?" asked Barboncito.

"East of here, where you will be protected."

Barboncito shook his head. "We were told this was a good land," he countered. "A place where there were trees to build our hogans, land to plant our crops and live in peace. But it was a lie. This is not a good place to live. There are no trees. The water isn't fit to drink or the land to farm. Many of our people have died of disease, cold, and hunger. We do not want to go to some reservation for the white man's government to protect us. We want to go home, where we can protect ourselves. We want to go back to our own sacred mountains and our gods."

General Sherman had a decision to make, and he needed time to think it over and talk with his committee.

THE NEW MEXICAN.

MANDERFIELD & TUCKER,
Editors and Proprietors.

SANTA FE, TUESDAY, JUNE 9, 1868.

For President,
ULYSSES S. GRANT,
of Illinois.

For Vice President,
SCHUYLER COLFAX,
of Indiana.

☞ The New Mexican is the largest sheet and has the largest circulation of any paper in New Mexico.

Lieut. Gen Sherman and the Navajos.

Lieut. General SHERMAN of the Indian Commission, arrived in this city on Friday evening last, from the Bosque Redondo, in company with Major General GETTY, where he had been to investigate the condition of the Navajos. From a gentleman of this city who has seen and conversed with the Lieut. General on the subject we learn that it has been determined to remove those Indians at once back to their native country. General SHERMAN has made an arrangement with them to go upon a reservation in their country, the boundaries of which are clearly defined; they to remain thereon, and pursue their pastoral and agricultural avocations; the government agreeing to give annnally to each member of the tribe a sum in wool, or other articles necessary, to five dollars, and secure them against the intrusion of whites. If the Navajos act in good faith, the government is to assist them in their efforts to sustain themselves; if they do not, then the United States is to withdraw its material aid and enforce obedience to the agreement entered into.

Newspaper article discussing the Navajo Peace Treaty and the relocation of the tribe. From *The New Mexican*, June 9, 1868.

"I will think about it," he promised. "I will do what I can to send you back to your own country."

"It does not matter whether the Navajo are sent east or back to their own country, as far as the government is concerned," Sherman told himself. "As long as they keep the peace and stop raiding, why not send them back to their own country, within the limits of a restricted area? They are in such poor condition and have multiplied so quickly that it will not take long for them to die out back in their rockbound canyons and high mesas. But at least they will be where they want to be."

The more General Sherman thought about sending them back to the arid Four Corners area, where Arizona, New Mexico, Colorado, and Utah country met, the more he liked the idea. "Something has to be done with the Navajo," he told the committee when they met. "These people already have cost the government far too much money. Next year, even though they work hard, they cannot possibly raise enough food on this alkaline soil to feed over 5,000 people.

"If we leave them here, they will die. If we send them east, the Plains Indians will make life so miserable for them that they will scatter, which will mean more trouble. I recommend they be allowed to return to their own country, provided they agree to stop their raids and keep the peace. The land in the Four Corners area is practically worthless. But they will cause less trouble there, now that they have learned their lesson; and it will cost the government less money to rebuild their flocks and maintain them until they can once again become self-supporting. Articles can be inserted into the treaty to prevent them from interfering with the building of a railroad across their land."

After much debating and many questions, a treaty was drafted to set aside 100 square miles of Navajo country in

Group of Navajo with Governor W. F. M. Arny, Navajo agent at Fort Defiance, Arizona, 1874–1875. Courtesy Smithsonian Institution National Anthropological Archives.

the Four Corners area, as far away from white settlements as possible. The government would help the Navajo to rebuild their flocks of sheep, provide them with seeds and tools, and maintain them for ten years or until they became self-supporting.

It is said that when finally General Sherman emerged from this meeting, the People ran to him, men, women, and children crying, "My Father! My Mother! Send us back to our own country! We want to go home!"

"Go slowly," he told them, embarrassed. "God have pity on you. I will meet with your headmen and see what can be done."

On June 1, 1868, the Navajo leaders assembled to listen to the terms of the treaty. It was a wordy document and took time to interpret. Briefly, it stated, among other things, that a tract of land measuring 100 square miles in the northwestern part of New Mexico and the northeastern part of what is now Arizona would be set aside for the Navajo tribe, provided its members agreed to give up raiding and to make a living at farming and sheep raising. In such case, each family would be allowed to own and cultivate 160 acres of its own choosing, and each child over 18 years of age, boy or girl, would be given eight acres of land to cultivate for his or her own use.

Each family also would be alloted $5 a year for clothing materials—$100 a year for seeds and farm implements. The tribe would also receive 15,000 sheep and goats, with which to rebuild its flocks, but not to eat. In addition, the tribe would be provided with food and other necessities for ten years if its members stayed on their own land and did not interfere with the building of a railroad across their land or destroy the buildings, harm the workers, or molest or carry off women or children along the line of trackage.

Articles of a Treaty and Agreement made and entered into at Fort Sumner New Mexico on the first day of June 1868, by and between the United States represented by its Commissioners Lieutenant General W. J. Sherman and Colonel Samuel J. Tappan of the one part, and the Navajo Nation or tribe of Indians represented by their Chiefs and Head men duly authorized and empowered to act for the whole people of said Nation or tribe (the names of said chiefs and Head men being hereto subscribed) of the other part, witness:—

Article. I

From this day forward all war between the parties to this agreement shall for ever cease. The Government of the United States desires peace, and its honor is hereby pledged to keep it. The Indians desire peace and they now pledge their honor to keep it.

If bad men among the whites or among other people, subject to the authority

Handwritten article of the Navajo Peace Treaty and signatures of General Sherman and another peace commissioner and of Navajo chiefs on the treaty document. Courtesy of General Services Administration, National Archives and Records Service, Washington, D.C.

the Territory of New Mexico set their
hands and seals.

W. T. Sherman
Lt Genl,
          Indian Peace Commissioner
S. F. Tappan,
          Indian Peace Commissioner

Barboncito. Chief   his X mark
~~Delgadito~~   ~~his X mark~~
Armijo   his X mark
   Delgado

Manuelito   his X mark
Largo   his X mark
Herrero   his X mark
Chiqueto   his X mark
Muerto de Hombre   his X mark
Hombro   his X mark
Narbono   his X mark
Narbono segundo   his X mark
Ganado Mucho   his X mark

                  Council

After each article was read, the leaders were asked if they understood its contents. Still acting as spokesman, Barboncito said, this time in his own tongue to his own people, "Let us give up our faults and go back to our own country without them. They brought us no sympathy. We have gained nothing."

The other chieftains agreed, and the answer was always, "Yes." They would have agreed to almost anything just then for an opportunity to go back to their own sacred mountains even though it was only about one-fourth of the territory they previously had called their own.

It was a dramtic moment when ten officers of the United States Army and 29 Navajo headmen signed the Treaty of Peace that day. The treaty not only ended four years of hopeless suffering, deprivation, and death, but it also brought to an end years of constant fighting between the Navajo and the invading white settlers and gave the Navajo a new lease on life.

12. A New Beginning

MANY CHANGES HAD taken place during the Navajos' exile. After the Civil War, the United States, all thirty-seven of them, had agreed to live in peace with one another. The Utes had been confined to a reservation; and a group of white men, known as Mormons, had taken over the Utes' country.

The Navajo knew nothing of these changes. They knew only that they were going home. Humbled, they were free now to return to their arid deserts, high mesas, and rockbound canyons—the land of the four sacred mountains. "The Happy Land," as Barboncito put it. "The land of the Diné! The People!"

On June 15, 1868, 50 ox-drawn army wagons, loaded with supplies, left Fort Sumner, with some 6,000 Navajo plodding along behind. Behind them plodded some 1,000 horses and 1,000 sheep they had managed to save during their four years at the Bosque.

The ten-mile caravan was flanked on each side by four companies of cavalry, whose mission was not only to protect and feed the people, but also to provide transportation for the sick, the young, and the aged.

It took two months to make the long trek back, but

it did not seem quite as long as it had four years ago, for this time the Navajo were going home.

One wagon in the midst of the canvas-covered caravan stood out like a huge black bird—a shiny, black buckboard with a lone passenger. Agent Dodd, of the Indian service, the Big Gopher, as the Navajo called him, was making his headquarters at Fort Defiance to look after their interest.

When finally the caravan reached Fort Wingate, the last stopping place before they reached the reservation, the Navajo were instructed to make camp. Technically, they were free. The bluecoats were no longer in charge and returned to Fort Sumner. Agent Dodd was in charge now, and he explained to the Navajo leaders that they would be held at Fort Wingate until surveyors had established the boundaries of their new reservation and Fort Defiance had been refurbished.

It was difficult for the Navajo to understand why this delay was necessary. They were eager to begin a new life in their old haunts, but they made the best of it. There was nothing else they could do.

It was November before the Navajo were allowed to return to their homeland. By then the weather had turned cold, and there were flurries of snow before they reached Fort Defiance. The men had been outfitted in old army coats and breetches; and the women and children, in cotton garments and warm blankets.

Fort Defiance did not look the same to them, however.

A small schoolhouse, warehouse, blacksmith's shop, carpenter's shop, and an agency building had been erected, as well as an adobe-walled corral and a small church for those who wished to attend.

By now winter had set in. The Navajo were instructed

to camp near the fort. Some of them lived in discarded army tents; some, in makeshift hogans. A few sheltered in shallow, wind-cut caves in the Bonito Hills, where an ancient tribe of Pueblo had once lived. Others scattered and sought their old haunts, some in the Canyon de Chelly. There was an abundance of wood here and pure water.

The northern boundary line of the new reservation lay along the same line as their old territory. It did not extend as far south, east or west, but it did include the slopes of the Chuska Mountains and the Canyon de Chelly.

The weather was extremely cold that winter. The snow was so deep that the promised sheep or supplies did not arrive. It was impossible for oxen to pull heavily loaded freight wagons across 800 miles of snow-covered plains from Fort Leavenworth, Kansas, to the Raton Pass, then shift the freight to packmules to complete the journey. Nor could the sheep travel through such deep snow.

Agent Dodd made every effort to keep the Navajo fed, but he was just one of many agents who failed to procure promised supplies. The Navajo did not complain, though. They had not forgotten how to dig for piñon nuts or nourishing roots. Moreover, the men, knowing the habits of every creature that lived in this rockbound country, had not forgotten how to catch rabbits, prairie dogs, and other rodents with curved sticks or slingshots. The People were not unhappy.

Even though they were not quite as free to roam as in the past, they were free to live their lives in their own way and to worship their own gods. Never again could men destroy their crops, kill their stock, or capture their women or children.

There was much to be done before spring arrived. Homesites had to be selected with the assistance of agent, and the promised 160 acres of land had to be staked out and recorded in the "land book" before new hogans could be built. Then, too, the long-neglected fields and orchards had to be cleared; and water holes, cleaned out.

An attempt was made that winter to comply with the terms of the treaty regarding the education of the children. A teacher, the wife of Dr. Mensul, who served as both doctor and pastor, set up classes in the new schoolhouse; and word was sent out for the children to attend. Only a few showed up. When the food and clothing that had been donated gave out, they scattered; and all effort to bring them back failed.

The first soft breath of spring brought back the Navajos' eagerness to till the soil and plant their crops, but there were not enough tools or seeds at the fort for every family to plant a full crop. They managed to keep busy, however. Shrines of stones and minerals had to be rebuilt before they could once again sing their prayer songs to the Holy Ones and perform their ceremonial rites. The medicine men gathered seeds, wild plants, and as much precious corn pollen as possible for their medicine pouches that summer and semiprecious stones for their sand paintings.

Several of the men worked at carpentry and blacksmithing when they were not hunting for game or wild horses. Those who had studied silversmithing under Juan Ares before the exile turned to iron, tin, or copper forging. The Navajo were a thrifty tribe. Nothing was ever wasted, and they soon learned that discarded barrel hoops could be made into shearing shears; that scraps of brass, copper wire, and bits of tin could be turned into bracelets or other simple ornaments. A bellows was made from a discarded goatskin. Tongs were made of scrap iron, and a tool to scratch out patterns was made from a discarded file.

These simple tools and the desire to learn were the beginning of Navajo silversmithing, a craft that later became recognized throughout the continent as one of the most beautiful primitive arts.

A few young men were taught how to gather healing herbs and the art of sand painting under the able direction of some elderly medicine man. The first paintings were abstract designs representing the sun, moon, or rainbow. They were made of crushed blossoms or other vegetable matter and dry pigments of colored rocks gathered from the Painted Desert west of the reservation.

After the colored rocks were ground into a coarse sand, they were dribbled onto a flat background of natural-colored sand from one to 20 feet in size. Actual symbols used in ceremonial rites were not taught to beginners. Only medicine men could paint healing pictures, administer healing herbs, or perform ceremonial rites.

Since the women had only a few sheep to tend that first summer and a very little bit of wool to spin, they spent their idle time in making a supply of baskets and pottery for everyday use. It is said that these baskets were so woven that only a few minutes of soaking in water made them watertight.

The art of making pottery was more difficult. It required certain clays that, when mixed with water, could be worked by hand into a stiff dough, then molded into various shapes and sizes such as bowls, pitchers, jugs, and bottles. These were then placed upside down on flat rocks in a pit of hot coals made of piñon wood. Juniper branches were spread over the hot coals to keep in the heat until the clay was completely fired. The pottery was then scraped smooth with a corncob or bone scraper and dyed. The dyes were made of the roots, leaves, and twigs of various plants that carried out the colors of the four sacred mountains.

Some historians say the Navajo learned how to weave baskets and mold pottery from the Pueblo, but others discard this theory. American Indians, regardless of tribe or location, had learned of necessity how to weave baskets and mold pottery to fit their needs many hundreds of years ago.

The long-awaited supplies did not arrive until the fall of 1869. By then several Navajo who had escaped to other territory during Kit Carson's tour of destruction returned to the reservation to receive their share of the land and the sheep that had been promised in the treaty.

Agent Dodd was not there to receive the supplies when they arrived. He had died early in the year. Mexican herders had driven the sheep to Fort Defiance; army men had received them and summoned the Navajo to the distribution.

Since there still was no interpreter other than Soos, the distribution lasted several days. The foodstuffs and other commodities were handed out first. The distribution of the 15,000 sheep and 1,500 goats was held until the last. Some of the allotted sheep and goats had died or been stolen along the trail. But enough were left to give each member of a family two sheep and one goat.

Before the crowd dispersed that day, Barboncito climbed to the top of the adobe-walled corral to make a speech. He was growing old now, but age had not impaired his power of oratory. He still had things to say, and he said them.

"Now that you have received a new start in sheep raising, take care of the sheep as you would your own children," he warned. "No matter how hard times are or how hungry you may be, never kill one. These sheep must grow into great flocks so that you can become as strong and powerful as you once were."

Barboncito's words were never forgotten. Even though the Navajo had never made a practice of killing sheep for food, they realized how important these sheep were and promised themselves to protect them with their lives.

From then on, ration day was once a month. Practically the whole tribe assembled at the fort to receive the beans, bacon, cornmeal, and other commodities handed out to them in emptied flour sacks.

Barboncito died during the 1870s. Ganado Mucho, a man of peace, was elected to take his place as spokesman.

The election of General Grant as president of the United States in 1869 had ushered in a new concept of how to handle Indian affairs. New policies were being adopted that it was hoped would bring about a better relationship between the federal government and all Indian tribes. One of the president's first acts was to promote Lieutenant General Sherman to a full generalship and give him command of the United States armies.

No one realized more than the general the importance of effective communication between the federal government and the Indians, especially the Navajo. On the local level, he encouraged the Navajo leaders and army personnel at Fort Defiance to meet once a month to discuss the Indians' tribal problems and objectives. After several of these meetings, the sessions were called chapters and became so popular that the movement spread, until meetings were held in various parts of the reservation to talk things over. The Navajo were a united tribe now. The new agent appointed Manuelito and Ganado Mucho as subchiefs to carry on these chapter meetings, Manuelito for the east side of the mountains and Ganado Mucho for the west.

The coming of the railroad also meant important changes in the lives of the Navajo. On May 10, 1869, two locomotives, the Jupiter and Number 119, stood nose to nose near the northern end of the Great Salt Lake, and a golden spike was driven joining the two ends of the tracks; this marked the completion of the first transcontinental railroad. Important men such as the president and General Sherman considered it the first link in a chain of better communication between the East and the West and of a better understanding between white men and Indians. But at that time it did not mean anything to the Navajo.

Owing to dry weather, their crops did not turn out well in 1870. Army rations had to be continued. They did not feel that their efforts were wasted, however, nor did they bemoan their loss. New orchards had been planted, and the sheep already were beginning to increase.

13. Gradual Progress

The first trading post was established at Fort Defiance in 1871. The shelves, stocked with many kinds of foods the Navajo had never heard of, with tin buckets and lanterns and other goods hanging from the ceiling, amazed them.

The parade ground became a place where they assembled on ration days to trade an extra piece of pottery, a basket, blanket, or horse for colored beads, a steel knife, or silver coin that could be melted down and worked into jewelry.

After Barboncito's death, Ganado Mucho stood on the wall to remind the People that they had made a promise not to steal or kill and that they must work for what they wanted. Ganado Mucho, chieftain of a western band living in the Chinle Valley, did all he could to bring about a better understanding between the Navajo and the Anglo-Americans.

As the sheep increased, grazing became a problem. The boundary lines of the arid, cactus-covered, rockbound land the government had doled out to the Navajo did not include enough grazing land to support their growing herds.

The men in Washington connected with Indian affairs had taken General Sherman's appraisal literally—

that the Navajo were a sickly lot and would soon die out. It was not long before the sheep and the herders began to drift to their old grazing grounds. Those who wandered east to the Checkerboard area* were disappointed. By now Mexican and Anglo-American sheepmen had taken over this area and fenced in the best water holes. This, of course, created clashes between the Navajo and white sheepherders.

While the sheep belonged to the women and it was their job to tend them, wash the wool, spin it into yarn, and dye it before weaving it into colorful blankets, the men helped with the shearing. They also took over when there was trouble and did the fighting.

The sheep increased rapidly, and before long the women had all the wool to spin they could handle. As in the past, they had no set patterns. No two designs were exactly alike. They not only were fine weavers, but their colorful patterns soon caught the eye of the trader. He bought their blankets as fast as they were completed and sold them to the wives of the army officers. Soon Navajo blankets became known throughout New Mexico and southern Utah for their fine quality. Agent Miller, who replaced the agent Dodd after the latter's death, also did his best to help the Navajo. He suggested that they sell part of their wool to carpet manufacturers in the East. The women agreed, and he soon found a market for the raw wool and taught the men how to bale it by the hundred-weight and ship it by oxcart to Santa Fe.

But trouble was brewing in the Checkerboard area. Disputes over water rights had always been a problem. They now developed into open warfare. Bottleggers also had entered the area and were trading the Navajo bad

---

* An uncharted area in New Mexico Territory adjoining the old Navajo land on the east. The Navajo and the Apache disputed the ownership of this land for many years, and, later, disputes arose between the Indians and the white settlers.

whiskey for sheep and horses. There had long been a law against selling liquor to Indians, but this did not stop the bootleggers.

In the past, the Navajo had not made or seemed to care for intoxicating liquors. The Spaniards had made grape wine and drunk it freely. The Apaches had made a corn drink they called tulapai. Now that whiskey was available, however, the Navajo often traded a fine horse for a bottle of bad whiskey. After the trade was made, they were forced to drink the liquor immediately and return the bottle so that no evidence of the illicit trade could be found.

Unable to cope with the situation, the Navajo leaders asked for help. Until then, they had never felt the need of organizing. In the past, their system of religious taboos had seemed all that was necessary; but now that more and more Anglo-American customs were being forced upon them, a unified code of law and the means of enforcing it were necessary.

A chapter meeting was called. After much discussion, a Navajo police force was organized. The governor of New Mexico even offered to train and equip ten strong young Navajo men for this purpose, under the agent's direction. For the first time in Navajo history a means of controlling offenders by tribal authority was in effect. Manuelito was placed in command of the ten-man police force. These men were the beginning of an organization that was later to become very powerful.

To help the situation, the government at Washington set aside a large section of grazing land for the Navajo, most of it west of the old boundary.

There still was a great deal of violence, however. Agent Miller was killed during a skirmish in 1872, and Thomas Keam, a special agent, took over his duties. By then the Navajo, for the first time in their lives, were receiving money from the sale of raw wool, blankets, and horses. Many of them could buy or trade now for guns, ammunition, tools, or a few extras they needed. The silversmiths could purchase more silver to work with. Atsidi Sani, who had worked with silver before the exile, also was one of the first to experiment with setting tourquoise stones in silver rings, bracelets, and neckpieces.

There still were only a few school buildings scattered over the hundreds of miles of reservation. Only those few children who happened to live near a schoolhouse attended. Schools did not mean anything to the Navajo at that time. Their interest was in planting and tending their crops and their sheep and in building new hogans. They were not interested in having their children learn how to speak English, to figure, or to write. Moreover, the Board of Foreign Missions, which the government had allowed to proselytize the Indians, was finding it difficult to persuade teachers to live in such isolated areas.

The special agent Keam was replaced by F. B. Arny, acting governor of New Mexico, who in 1874 assumed charge of the agency. Several Navajo were killed during a raid in the old Ute country that year. The blame was placed on local Mormons. It is said that the agent Arny used this incident to convince the commissioner of Indian Affairs that warfare between the Navajo and the Mormons was imminent. The Navajo denied this.

In August, Arny asked permission to accompany a delegation of Navajo leaders to Washington to protest the stealing of their sheep in Utah and in the Checkerboard area; but some people believed that Arny's real motive in going to Washington was to effect a land exchange by ceding Navajo land along the northern border, where goldseekers already were staking out claims, for less valuable land in the Checkerboard area. Although Thomas Keam had been replaced by Arny, he joined the delegation at his own expanse to look after the Navajos' interest.

President Grant met with the delegation on December 10, 1874. When the Navajo, with the help of Thomas Keam, explained to the president that they did not want to exchange their land for less desirable land in the Checkerboard area and that they wanted a stop put to Anglo-Americans' and Mexicans' stealing their sheep and fencing off the water holes, the president promised them that the land exchange would not go through.

During this period, John D. Lees built a ferry across the Colorado River not far above the Grand Canyon and established a trading post there to deal with the Indians. He did not own the land the post occupied; few traders did. But it was a large post, consisting of a good-sized, adobe store building; a barn; a warehouse; and corrals for both sheep and horses. A roomy hogan was also built to accommodate visiting Indians who had traveled a long way.

A trader in Indian country had to be a shrewd man and able to speak several languages and Indian tongues. Since many of the Indians from various tribes had very little, if any, cash to spend, trader Lees established a credit system so that the Navajo could pawn their trinkets and blankets until shearing time. Soon other traders, learning of the valuable blankets and silver jewelry the Navajo were turning out, came to the reservation to trade. The presence of these white traders opened up a new world to the Navajo, and shortly thereafter other trading posts outside the reservation were established.

In 1874, the government issued $40,000 worth of cotton shirts, trousers, coats, and vests to the Navajo men and cotton garments to the women and children. Not long after that, buckskin and leather garments began to disappear. The Navajo now wore ready-made garments or clothing made of flour sacks, unbleached muslin, denim, or flowered calico.

The prosperity of the Navajo created a great deal of antagonism between them and the Anglo-Americans. Each time the government gave the Indians more grazing land that had once been public domain, the homesteaders became more belligerent. The Navajo could have homesteaded a claim like anyone else had this privilege been explained to them. Instead of homesteading more land and living on it, they continued to move their flocks to fresh grazing grounds several times a year and to erect temporary hogans. There is no record of their homesteading land other than their original 160 acres between the years of 1868 and 1905.

Surveyors for the Central Railroad, later called the Santa Fe, entered the reservation in 1875 to map out a route for the tracks. The railroad from the East had already reached Albuquerque and was scheduled to pass through Fort Wingate and on to Arizona.

When the Navajo learned that the tracks would pass through some of their best grazing land and destroy some of their finest water holes, they were horrified. It was true they had promised not to hinder the building of the railroad or molest its property or people, but they could not just sit back and let it take over so much of their best land.

Agent Arny was forced to resign in August 1875. A new agent was appointed who agreed to accompany Manuelito, Ganado Mucho, and six other Navajo chiefs to Washington, D.C. They rode by buckboard to Independence, Missouri, then by train to Washington. The capital was in an uproar at that time over the forthcoming presidential election, but the Navajo were treated with courtesy. After they explained their problem to the superintendent of Indian affairs, they were reminded of the treaty they had signed. It was then explained to them why the railroads needed extra land, not only for a right-of-way on each side of the tracks, but also for small settlements to be built where passengers and freight could be dispersed and where wool, blankets, and horses could be sent to eastern markets almost from their front door.

"But the tracks will take in miles of our most valuable land," Manuelito protested. "We will need more grazing ground."

He was then assured that a strip of land north of the San Juan River would be given to them in lieu of the land they had relinquished. And true to the superintendent's word, nearly a million acres were granted to the Navajo, extending their reservation into and past Hopi Indian country.

The ten-year period of government assistance ended in 1878. It had been a difficult period, but a rewarding one. From a sick, destitute people, the Navajo had become an industrious, prosperous tribe that also had doubled in numbers. At that time they owned some 20,000 horses, several thousand goats, and over 100,000 sheep.

The homesteaders and government agencies in the Southwest thought the government in Washington had given the Navajo too much land. They did not realize that most of it was covered with cactus and yucca—land no white settler would live on.

During this period, antogonism between the Navajo and the Anglo-Americans continued. Raids against Mexican settlements in the Zuñi area also became more frequent. They reached such proportions that Manuelito and Ganado Mucho decided to carry out a purge on some so-called witches they considered were causing all the trouble. This "purge" did not stop the raids.

The police force continued to operate; however, now

that the Navajo had doubled in numbers and occupied almost twice as much land as they had before the exile, such a small force could not handle the situation. A company of scouts was organized in an effort to control the increasing raids, but it lasted only a year.

The most disappointing failure during this ten-year period, however, was the failure to maintain enough schools. The Navajo and the government were both responsible. Evidently, the government had no idea that the Navajo were spread out over 3,500,000 acres and that it was impossible for very many children to reach any one of the schools, even in the best of weather. Then too, school meant little more to the Navajo than a child's sitting on a bench all day when he could be herding sheep. Even at Fort Defiance, where there had been a school for the entire ten-year period, there were never more than eleven pupils at any one time. The agent's report in 1878 reminded those in charge of Indian affairs that while thousands of dollars had been spent on schools and teachers so far, not one Navajo could either read or write.

Conditions gradually changed, however. As the railroad tracks advanced beyond Fort Wingate, crews of Navajo were recruited to carry water, help clear the right-of-way, and do other unskilled jobs. The men that laid the ties for the rails were mostly cowboys, miners, and homesteaders who needed extra money. Most of them were heavy drinkers. Whiskey, railroad ties, and scrap iron soon began to influence the Navajos' way of life. After a piece of iron was tossed aside, it was picked up and carried to some hogan or a blacksmith, who found many uses for it. The discarded square-hewn railroad ties, when laid on top of each other, made several-sided hogans with six to eight rooms. Or they could be stood upright and covered with a flat roof. Soon hogans made of railroad ties could be seen, not only along the tracks in every direction, but also in many isolated places.

As the tracks advanced deeper and deeper into Navajo country, settlements sprang up along the right-of-way. These included a trading post, a saloon and a depot, where freight trains, their small engines belching smoke from a huge stack, stopped to disperse passengers from a caboose at the rear or discharge freight from cars that opened on the side. When the train reached the end of the track, where crews were laying fresh rails, it returned the way it had come, as there was only one set of tracks.

Raw wool, sheep, horses, silver jewelry, and colorful blankets were being shipped to eastern markets almost from the Navajos' back door. The silver jewelry became so popular that traders began to stock better tools for the silversmiths, such as gasoline blowtroches and dies to stamp out more intricate patterns. Atsidi Sani and his sons soon had several apprentices working under them to take over much of the rough work. Sani also brought several skilled Mexican silversmiths to the reservation to teach those who wanted to learn. He bought most of his silver in Mexico as it was softer and more easily worked than silver dollars.

Most of the Navajo were devoting their time to sheep raising, however. The government instructed the agents to look into the possibility of introducing Merion and Rambouille rams into the flocks to improve the quality and quantity of the wool.

A few of the more influential Navajo became established on land where the range was consistently good in most years, but the majority of the Navajo had to seek good range land beyond their own homesites. To do this, they had to move from place to place, where grazing was more plentiful.

As the sheep and horses increased, the grazing lands

became depleted. The herders had to find grazing land farther and farther away from the reservation. When the chieftains asked for more land, two more strips, 15 miles wide along the southern and eastern borders of the reservation, were given back to them.

14. The Railroad

THE 1880s WERE wild and troublesome years. The coming of the railroad not only disturbed the Navajo, it also brought a criminal element, armed with Winchester rifles and six-shooters, that ran riot over most of the Southwest. It also brought prosperity. Land values boomed. Thousands of white Americans swarmed into New Mexico and Arizona to homestead large ranches and homesites or go into business.

Many adjustments had to be made by both the Navajo and the Anglo-Americans during these years, and the adjustments were not always easy.

The first train reached Fort Wingate in 1881, then moved on to a stop called Gallup, where a depot was established and a telegraph office as well. Until the surveyors had laid out a route for the tracks, Gallup had been only a way-stop for the Overland Stage line. Soon it became a thriving settlement, where wool, sheep, and horses could be shipped East and where supplies for Fort Defiance and the trading post were picked up by oxcart and the mail delivered by a mounted policeman from the fort twice weekly.

From Gallup, the tracks dipped slightly south, then

west to Winslow and Flagstaff. The first stop west of Gallup, however, was called Ferry Station, which later was
renamed Manuelito. A spur line also ran north from Gallup
to a coal mine about halfway to the fort. No passengers
were allowed to travel on this line, however, other than
coal miners, a few sheep buyers, or Indians. They rode in a
caboose at the end of the train, where they could sit on
benches or sleep on the floor. During the winter a small
wood-burning stove was installed to keep them warm.

The first piece of modern machinery to reach the
reservation was a small ten-horsepower sawmill. It was set
up north of the fort in the Fluted Rock area, where timber
was plentiful. The lumber was to be used for a three-story
boarding school and a mission at the fort. The logs had to
be skidded to the mill by oxteam and the lumber hauled to
the fort by this same method.

It seemed to Manuelito, a shrewd man, that there
should be a better means of transporting lumber and supplies than by oxcart. With the agent's assistance, he ordered
a dozen sturdy farm wagons sent to the trading post. When
they arrived, he soon learned how to harness his largest
and gentlest horses and hitch them to one of the wagons.

Ganado Mucho, the "Peace Chief," also bought a
wagon and learned how to harness his horses and handle
the reins. The railroad crossed his land in the Chinle Valley, almost due west of Gallup. He earned over a hundred
dollars during that first year hauling supplies from Gallup
to the fort and trading post.

Ganado Mucho knew how to take advantage of opportunity when it came. Realizing that his land was ideally
situated for a settlement and supplied with plenty of water,
he encouraged his friend Don Lorenzo Hubbell to build a
trading post near the tracks that continued on to Winslow
and Flagstaff. He also promised Hubbell a large trade from

his own people as well as any trade the passengers would bring him.

Don Lorenzo Hubbell was so grateful for this opportunity that he named the settlement Ganado and did everything in his power to serve the people in that area. When necessary, he served as doctor, undertaker, adviser, or peacemaker. After a depot was established at Ganado, the trading post prospered and in time became a national historical site.

Winslow became district headquarters for the Santa Fe Railroad, but civilization came to Winslow with the building of the first Harvey House restaurant. While the wood and coal-burning engine took on fuel and water, the passengers could leave the train to stretch or dine on fine food, which was served on white table linens by neatly uniformed young ladies.

The boarding school and mission at Fort Defiance were completed in 1883; both were managed by missionaries. Only eighty-four pupils enrolled, however. The Navajo were still superstitious about letting their children leave home and live with white Anglo-Americans. As far as most of them were concerned, the Anglo-Americans were still their enemies. Their flocks of sheep were steadily increasing; the children were needed at home to protect them from predators.

To the dismay of those in charge, the children who had enrolled did not like the school. They were not allowed to speak their native tongue or wear tribal clothing. Unable to understand English, they were often whipped for some infraction of rules they did not understand, deprived of their meals, or locked in rooms. Navajo children were not accustomed to being punished. They were always treated with love and kindness. Frightened, they climbed out of school windows and set out for home. Sometimes it took them several days to reach their homes. It was reported that one girl died of exposure and that one boy's feet were frozen. After that, the windows were barred at both the school and the mission; mistreatment of the pupils continued.

By then the Navajo had increased in numbers to about 19,000. Their horses had increased to about 35,000; their goats, to some 200,000; and their sheep, to 1,000,000. Again a call went out for more land. By 1884 all of the land in southern Utah below the San Juan River had been restored to the Navajo. Their sheep, horses, and goats could now graze from the San Juan to the Little Colorado and from the Rio Grande valley to the Grand Canyon.

The more affluent Navajo were now building log houses, some with two rooms, instead of stick and mud hogans. Tin buckets and metal pans were replacing home-made jugs and cooking utensils. The traders also were stocking manufactured dyes in small packages, so that Navajo women no longer had to make their own. The women also could now buy warp and weft finer than what they could spin with their own yarn. Moreover, since they could sell their beautiful handmade rugs and blankets to the Harvey House as fast as they could weave them, they no longer wore their own blankets. Instead, they wore government-issue cotton garments.

By then Harvey Houses all along the Santa Fe line were adding display rooms, where Navajo crafts could be sold. The sliversmiths also had discarded most of their handmade tools for precise manufactured instruments and melted their silver in molds etched with their own designs instead of designs of Spanish origin. By then rings, buckles, buttons, neckpieces, and other ornaments, embellished with beautiful turquoise stones, began to appear and sold at a good price.

In an effort to keep Navajo parents from interfering with their children's attending school, the Indian Bureau enforced a compulsory school act. This did not always work, however. Sometimes when a truant officer drove up to a hogan, the children were hidden or ran away by themselves. When the parents were forced to send a child to school, they sent only the weakest or sickly children. The healthy ones were kept at home to tend the sheep.

Manuelito and other subchiefs made speeches explaining why it was necessary for the children to attend school. They said that it not only was the law, but that it was necessary for them to get an education. The children continued to run away, however. It seemed that no one, in those days, ever considered the idea of making schools a pleasant experience for the pupils. Even pupils in white schools were whipped for breaking the rules.

By 1890 Fort Defiance had developed into a substantial community. Many of the old buildings had been replaced by sawed lumber structures with glass windows and doors. The fort was now a center of activity and was called the Cradle of Progress. A law was enacted that same year that required all teachers to pass a civil service examination before they could acquire a license to teach. As the teachers became better qualified, more and more Navajo favored sending their children to school.

A new boarding school was also set up at Grand Junction, Colorado, that year to provide schooling for the children of all the Indian tribes in the Southwest. A matron and a doctor were on the staff. Not only were qualified teachers hired to teach the fundamentals, but artists and skilled craftsmen were also hired to teach the native arts and crafts.

In 1893 a new agent by the name of Plummer thought it a good idea to take some of the more advanced Navajo students to the world's fair in Chicago. Other agents in the Southwest were doing this to show the students how the more civilized peoples of the world lived and also to display their native crafts. The government did not pay for this trip. The Indian Rights Association, an organization that was becoming increasingly important in Indian affairs, footed the bill.

The Navajo youth were amazed by what they saw at the fair, especially when they met Indians from Alaska who spoke their own language. Their parents had never heard of, or had forgotten, the legend of the separation that had taken place centuries ago when some of the Diné, the totem pole Indians of Alaska, had stayed in the far north while the others had continued on south.

When the young people returned to the reservation and told of the many wonderful things they had seen at the fair and of meeting people who spoke their own language, Manuelito and several Navajo headmen decided to go to Chicago to see these wonders for themselves.

Manuelito died during the winter of 1893; but before his death, he called his people to him and told of the many wonderful things he had seen. "The white men have many things we Navajo need," he said, "but we cannot get them until we change our ways. My children, education is the ladder to all our needs. Tell our people to take it."

After Manuelito's death, the Navajo had no great leader to turn to as they had in the past. They went to the agent from then on for government help.

As recently as 1897, however, something happened that almost caused a war. Sixteen Navajo families were tending their sheep on land in a grazing district on the far side of the Colorado River—the Little Nile, as it was called—when several Anglo-American men rode up and demanded a $5 fee from each of the families for every one hundred sheep they owned.

The Navajo did not know what to do. They had no money to pay such a fee. When they asked for time to see what could be done, the men refused to listen. The Mormons were developing an irrigation system connected with the river and did not want Indians near.

A light snow was falling, and the ewes were lambing. These facts did not influence the men. They burned the hogans and corrals, then pushed the parents, children, and sheep toward the river, firing rifles and revolvers to hurry them along. The river was too deep for the lambs to swim. Nearly all of them drowned or froze to death.

The episode was finally smoothed over without a war, but the resentment against the Mormons was still there.

The craft of silversmithing did not really become commercial until 1899, when Fred Harvey ordered silver ornaments made expressly for the tourist trade. They were lighter and thinner than those the Navajo made for their own use. This jewelry sold for less money, but it was a lucrative craft, and the market was unlimited.

There were good years and bad years during the 1800s, but the Navajo had made a headstart in the white man's world. They continued to take advantage of what was important to them, as they had in the past, and discarded the rest.

Slowly but surely, the Navajo were changing from a fighting tribe to one of sheep raising and business. Never again would they return to their old way of living.

15. Dogged Perseverance

A BETTER RELATIONSHIP between the Navajo and the Anglo-Americans developed during the early 1900s. One of the worst stumbling blocks to a better understanding had been the constant political changes in Washington, D.C. Each new commissioner of Indian affairs had brought with him his own ideas and policies, which had confused the Navajo. But since most of the tribes had been confined to reservations and the Indian wars in the Southwest were over, the government now had time to consider the health, welfare, and education of the various Indian tribes.

In 1901 the Bureau of Indian Affairs placed an agent in each of the six districts of the Navajo reservation to investigate conditions there. Their reports disclosed that in the areas where grazing grounds were plentiful, several Navajo families owned over a thousand sheep and a great drove of idle horses. In the more isolated areas, where grazing land was scarce, the Navajo were poor. Their flocks of sheep were small, and they owned only a few horses.

Having an agent in each of the six districts had its good points, especially in the outlying districts, where travel was impossible other than on foot or horseback. This did not help to equalize the situation, however, or bring the tribe together as a whole.

In 1906 Congress appointed money for the building of several hospitals and schools for the Navajo and a modern sawmill in the Toadlena area to provide lumber for the building of these establishments. In the meantime, a day school, mission, and small hospital were built by a religious group at Ganado; and in a short time, day schools were established at Toadlena, Tuba City, Crownpoint, and Shiprock.

Several boarding schools were also established outside the reservation. Educators were convinced that schools farther away, now that there were better roads, were more practical than schools nearer the pupils' homes. These new school buildings not only had the number of prescribed classrooms, but they had indoor laboratories, bathrooms, and laundries. Even sewing machines were provided so that the students could learn how to sew. An Indian housekeeper prepared a midday meal and taught them how to use the new facilities. They also were taught how to develop their native arts and crafts and other cultural aspects.

In 1911 Congress passed a resolution conferring statehood on Arizona, and New Mexico was considered tame enough by 1912 to admit to the Union.

The automobile made its first appearance on the reservation in 1915. The battered jalopy amused the Navajo. As far as they were concerned, this box on wheels was not practical—it could not multiply. Sheep and horses were much more useful. Later, they were forced to transfer some of their love for horses to motored vehicles, but not yet.

When the United States entered World War I in 1917, the United States government was amazed that hundreds of Navajo youth enlisted to help their country, as no Indians were drafted. Many of these youths distinguished themselves by their bravery and after the war the president extended recognition to the Navajo tribe for the loyalty and patriotic service its members had rendered. Members of other Indian tribes had also enlisted and made records of bravery. They too were cited.

By the 1920s the Navajo in the more populated areas were receiving a fair income from the sale of their handiwork. Their identity as a cultural group, distinct from that of other tribes, became a source of great pride. Notices of their fine craftsmanship began to appear in tourist brochures and more serious literature. It pleased them to know that they were becoming as well known as the Pueblo in Anglo-American society.

It still was necessary for the government to issue rations and other annuities to the Navajo families living in the isolated areas during dry seasons, however, when the range became depleted of forage for their flocks.

The discovery of oil in the Shiprock area in 1921 revealed the need for a tribal government. The question of who should sign the oil leases created some confusion. The Treaty of 1868 specified that before a crucial decision concerning the welfare of the tribe could be made, the consent of three-fourths of the people from all sections of the reservation must be obtained.

A meeting that was called to discuss this problem resulted in the first Navajo tribal council. Two men from each district were elected as candidates to speak for their people. The first tribal chairman to be elected was Henry Chee Dodge. His grandmother, a Pueblo, was one of the women sent to the Canyon de Chelly stronghold during the uprising of 1860. He had been raised at Fort Defiance and often acted as interpreter. He now was a prosperous sheepman and horseman and also a man of peace who had learned how to get along with the Anglo-Americans. His advice was always welcomed. When he told the Navajo, "Send your children to school to learn about farming and sheep raising" and "Take care of yourselves in the new way," they listened.

A vice-chairman and a treasurer were also elected to the council for a period of four years. These two men and the chairman signed the first oil leases.

The tribal council met annually after that to iron out tribal problems. As a result of good management from the income of the oil and gas leases, several irrigation ditches were dug in the dry areas, and additional educational opportunities were provided.

The improved methods of breeding and raising sheep through the Indian Agricultural Extension Service had increased the size of most flocks until the grazing land and water sources were becoming depleted in several districts. There no longer was enough grassland to feed the thousands of sheep and droves of idle horses. The once green pastures were eaten down to the bare earth, and the land eroded into deep gullies. When their stock began to die, the Indians did not understand what was happening. Nor did the farmers or stockmen all over the country realize that water, good soil, and grass were not something that continued to last without good care and proper management.

When Franklin Roosevelt took office as president of the United States in 1933, one of his first acts was to create several agencies: a Soil Conservation Service, a public works program, a relief administration, and others.

William H. Zeh, an Indian Bureau forester, was appointed by the Soil Conservation Service to investigate conditions on the Navajo reservation. After an intensive

Another great natural resource of the Navajo—the skill of their people. A Navajo grandmother prepares her yarn for weaving. Courtesy U.S. Department of the Interior, Bureau of Indian Affairs.

survey, he reported that owing to the uneven distribution of sheep and horses in certain areas the shortage of water and grassland had caused great stretches of eroded soil. He strongly recommended that a stock reduction program be put into effect immediately. He felt that the only solution was to have fewer grazing animals.

The tribal council understood the need for such a program, but it was a blow to those who had struggled for years to increase their stock. Large flocks of sheep and droves of horses meant wealth and prestige. They could not understand such a program.

It was not explained to the Navajo that the United States was in the throes of a vicious depression or that this same program affected every farmer and stock raiser in the country. Suspicion and resentment reached a high pitch when in the fall of 1933 a newly organized relief administration purchased 100,000 head of sheep from all sections of the reservation at one dollar a head, then shot them and left them to rot.

Several thousand horses were sold in order to conserve grazing land. Even as this was being done, Civilian Conservation Corps trucks, loaded with machinery and supplies, rolled across the sandy deserts of the reservation. Camps were set up, and word was sent out for workers. Soon hundreds of Navajo, accustomed to travel only on foot or horseback, were being taught how to drive trucks and tractors. Others were being taught how to handle pumping machines used to dig huge irrigation ditches, while still others were hired to build better roads. A few Navajo were selected to visit a laboratory near Fort Wingate to study the benefits of soil conservation and proper range management.

Under the president's order, the six districts of the reservation were once again thrown into one, and a general superintendent was temporarily put in charge of all. It was then suggested that the unification of all Navajo agencies be etsablished under one roof and that a site be selected for the construction of an administration building.

John Collier, commissioner of Indian Affairs, suggested that Window Rock be selected for the site. Tseghaodzani, or Perforated Rock as it was known, was a natural window under a high arch of rock carved out by the wind; it lay about halfway between Fort Defiance, Arizona, and Gallup, New Mexico. It had long been a sacred meeting place for Navajo ceremonial rites. The new building was constructed of red sandstone quarried in the vicinity, and it housed not only the tribal council, but also the offices of the Bureau of Indian Affairs and the Public Health Service. Later, a post office, a bank, and other buildings were erected.

The Reorganization Act, passed in 1934, allowed Window Rock to incorporate like any other city. In the meantime, the council had adopted a policy to encourage large firms in the field of electronics to build plants on the reservation. Until then, the lack of good roads had hampered the development of such utilities.

About this time, it was discovered that the interest on the money in oil and gas leases, deposited in the national treasury, had not been credited to the Navajos' account. An agent was sent immediately to Washington to investigate this discrepancy. The accumulated interest amounted to $200,000. The mistake was rectified. By 1935 more than $140,000,000 in interest, bonuses, leases, and royalties were deposited to the tribe's account.

In 1937 the council was reorganized in its present form of 74 delegates, a chairman, vice-chairman, and treasurer. The first ballots for the election of these officers had pictures of the candidates on them for those who could not read or write.

In the meantime, the Navajo Mounted Police Force was enlarged. By then the reservation covered more than 25,000 square miles. The Navajo, who had lived together for centuries without jails, orphanges, or welfare agencies, now felt the need of a strong police force.

By 1938 the Indian Office in Washington had reached the decision that it was time for the Navajo to learn how to read and write their own language. Dr. John Harrington of the Smithsonian Institution and Oliver La Farge, author and ethnologist, adapted the Roman alphabet to the sounds of the Indian language.

In 1940, John Adair, skilled in Indian crafts, founded the Arts and Crafts Guild. With the assistance of Ambrose Rainhorse, also a skilled craftsman, he maintained a high standard of both materials and workmanship.

When the United States entered World War II on December 7, 1941, several ammunition plants were set up in the Southwest near the reservation. Many Navajo, male and female, were hired for various types of work. It was well known that the Navajo not only were good workers, but had also made good soldiers during World War I. It also was well known that the Navajo language was the most difficult to understand or speak. Only about 20 non-Indians could either understand or speak it, and most of them were missionaries who had lived on the reservation for several years. Since there had never been a written language until Harrington and La Farge used the Roman alaphabet to record the Navajo language, there was no way that the Japanese or Germans could understand messages sent in the Navajo tongue. Until then, commanders in the South Pacific had been having trouble in preserving the secrecy of their communication system. The Navajo language was the solution.

During the year 1942, some 500 educated Navajo youth enlisted in the Fourth Marine Corps. Four hundred and twenty of them qualified as "Code Talkers" and were given intensive training stateside before being sent overseas.

The Navajos' part in the war was a guarded secret, however, until V. J. Day, when the story was told of how these "Code Talkers" had confounded the enemy with their unbreakable code in almost every operation from Sicily to the South Pacific, the Solomons, Marianas, Peleliu, and Iwo Jima. After the war, each of these young marines was cited for bravery and received a special medallion based on a painting of the Iwo Jima landing by Joe Ruiz Grandee.

In addition, thousands of other Navajo who, because of lack of education, did not qualify for military service, worked outside the reservation and did their part.

The work on road improvement and other projects was brought to a standstill during the war, but the work of the tribal council continued. Henry Chee Dodge was again elected tribal chairman in 1942, and Sam Ahkeah was elected vice-chairman and held that office until after Chee's death. He then served as chairman. During this time he conducted a survey of the minerals on the reservation that led to the discovery of new oil fields and uranium.

When the war was over, the men and women who had worked outside the reservation had a better understanding of the world and the importance of an education.

16. Years of Fulfillment

THE DISCOVERY OF uranium ore on the reservation led to a new industry that boosted the Navajos' economic level to the extent that expert advice was needed to handle the money pouring into the tribal council's office. A resident attorney was hired for this purpose.

The long-range Rehabilitation Act also helped such projects as a right-of-way for new power lines to be strung across the more heavily populated areas and the building of two-room homes made of lumber to replace more of the mud and stick hogans. The Stock Reduction Program also was revised, enabling the Navajo to enlarge their flocks of sheep, but not their horses. By then the pickup truck had practically replaced the horse for commercial purposes. Many families in the remote areas, however, still clung to the old ways of life.

An educational fund was established for honor students in 1951, and the Arts and Crafts Guild had grown so rapidly and become so popular that it was made a tribal enterprise.

A work program that guaranteed ten days work a month for those in need also became a tribal enterprise. So many projects were in the process of being developed by then that a Remington Rand expert was called to Window Rock to help establish an effective record system for the ever-growing files.

Plans for a fairground, which had been set aside during the war years, were now revived. A racetrack with grandstands for spectators and a rodeo center were constructed. Buildings and stalls also were constructed where tribal contests could be held, crafts and agricultural produce displayed, and livestock exhibited. Soon tourists from the East came to the reservation to enjoy the fair. And even though the fair became more modern through the years, the Navajo retained as much of the past as possible. The women continued to wear their bright, full-skirted dresses, bedecked with silver ornaments heavily studded with turqoise for the occasion, and the men wore Levi's, colorful shirts, and similar jewelry.

By 1953 most of the projects on the reservation were progressing—all but the health of the Navajo. The tribe numbered about 61,000, and there were not enough doctors or hospitals to take care of the sick. When this problem came to the attention of the Bureau of Indian Affairs, a large sum of money was allotted for the enlarging and the building of hospitals. By 1956, 17 different Christian sects were working on the reservation in collaboration with the Public Health Service.

Even the medicine men, after seeing what modern medicine could do, cooperated with the doctors. When they suspected a serious illness, they often recommended that the patient be sent to a hospital.

It was difficult at first for the Navajo to place their lives in the hands of white doctors. But gradually, as the combination of the Navajos' healing arts and the white doctors' medicine began to take effect, there were times when a medicine man and a doctor stood together beside the bed of a patient in harmony and good faith, each doing what he could to save a life.

Paradoxical as it may seem, the more the Navajo absorbed the white man's culture and the more parents were willing to send their children to school, the more pride they took in their own culture. Their tribal religion and other cultural values continued to be an important part of their lives.

Soon there were not enough schools, especially in the remote areas. Money was appropriated to remedy this situation in 1958. Day schools, boarding schools, parochial schools, and trailer schools began to appear over most of the 25,000 square miles of the reservation. The trailer schools, equipped with a small but modern classroom, bathroom, and kitchenette, could reach the most remote areas. Within a few years there were enough schools on the reservation to accommodate 95 percent of all school age children. Moreover, through the efforts of the Indian Bureau, a newspaper and other literature were being printed in the Navajo tongue.

By then a Navajo Tribal Parks Commission and a Navajo Rangers Department had been organized. Money was also appropriated for the construction of a large sawmill to be set up about 15 miles east of Fort Defiance. A stand of ponderosa pine in that area, estimated to be worth some $30 million was to be cut for the building of various projects. The Navajo Products Industry was built to turn the waste material into such by-products as bark and chips for landscaping and agricultural purposes, prefab houses, and pulp for paper mills.

The first large appropriation for water development was made in 1960. An irrigation system that had long been in the planning stage would, when completed, store and channel enough water from the San Juan River to irrigate

110,000 acres of arid wasteland and thereby transform the land into hundreds of profitable farms.

Work also was started on such projects as chapter houses, community centers, roadside rest stops, and bus shelters for the children. Branch offices for the Arts and Crafts Guild and other tribal agencies were also constructed in several of the more heavily populated areas. These programs not only gave hundreds of men employment, they also provided the necessary training they needed to procure work off the reservation through the Relocation Program.

By the fall of 1965 thousands of tourists were flowing to the Land of the Four Sacred Mountains, not only to attend the Navajo Fair, but to see and enjoy nature's lavish display of scenic wonders: the Grand Canyon, the Petrified Forest, the Canyon de Chelly, and many other fantastic rock formations—and they were welcome. Tribal parks, camping grounds, and hunting and fishing areas had been established for their comfort and pleasure. Tourists could now purchase beautiful handwoven rugs, blankets, jewelry, and other arts and crafts. Tourism in the Southwest was becoming big business, and the Navajo took advantage of it when possible.

The police force, which had grown steadily since its inception, was reorganized in 1968 with headquarters at Window Rock. A new law and order building had been constructed there with prison facilities, court rooms, and appointed judges, who presided over civil and minor criminal cases. A Navajo now had the privilege of having his case heard by a jury of his peers.

The first college to be established on an Indian reservation in the United States was the Navajo Community College. It was established by a resolution of the Navajo Tribal Council in August 1968 and opened its doors to students in January 1969 to provide them and the forthcoming generations with educational opportunities their ancestors never had. Because of lack of funds, the college utilized the facilities of the new Bureau of Indian Affairs high school at Many Farms, Arizona, until the money was appropriated for a seperate building. The college was, and still is, operated and controlled by the Navajo themselves.

The Navajo Community College offers a full two-year term of college courses for students who want to continue their education in some four-year college or university. It also emphasizes vocational techniques and adult educational courses. Non-Indian students may attend.

Dr. Ned A. Hatathli, president of the college, said, "The fullest growth of the Navajo reservation depends in a large part upon the availability of educated Navajos."

A quotation from the late Senator Robert Kennedy on the college's letterhead stationery reads: "Some men see things as they are and ask Why . . . I dream things that never were and ask why not." The college feels that this quotation is especially appropriate for the 130,000 Navajo, who, despite their average family income of approximately $680 per year, dared to reach for the stars and turn a dream into a reality.

The new college campus will be built on the shore of Lake Tsaile in one of the most beautiful portions of the reservation. In line with a mandate from the Board of Regents, the campus will reflect the dignity, beauty, and strength of Navajo culture. The new college will have a capacity of 1,500 students when all three phases of construction are completed.

Peter MacDonald, present chairman of the Navajo Tribal Council, said, in part, in his inaugural address on January 5, 1971,

Today, many eyes are upon us, for we are a people

of destiny, and we have reached one of the great turning points in the history of our people, and the history of all Indian people.

What we do now, this year and over the next years, will be watched not only on this Reservation ... by our neighbors, by Indians throughout this country, by Congress and by the White House. ... President Nixon said in his historic message of last July 8th, 'The time has come to break decisively with the past and to create the conditions for a new era in which the Indians' future is determined by Indian acts and Indian decisions.' President Nixon entrusted an Indian, Louis Bruce, [with] the direction of the Bureau of Indian Affairs, and Commissioner Bruce has been faithful to that mission.

One Hundred and Three years ago we returned from the Long Walk, 15,000 of us, to claim this reservation as our land. We have multiplied tenfold. We have endured hardship, discouragement and despair. We are destiny's children and we have endured as one People ... our past gave us the present, but the future is ours to forge. ...

We are a proud people, because we are sustained by our heritage, which teaches us great lessons. Essentially it tells us that planning and innovating without our Creator will lead to unhappiness, for the spiritual aspect of man gives us that hope.

Ready to begin forging that future, Chairman MacDonald pledged that, in response to the challenge defined by President Nixon, the Navajo would lead the way to self-sufficiency. He described the Navajo as looking to the future with hope and confidence, with vision and determination that would allow the tribe to continue on the path toward dignity, justice and a state of well-being while praying for happiness and for peace in their hearts and their minds.

Bibliography

Adair, John. *The Navajo and Pueblo Silversmiths.* Norman, Okla.: University of Oklahoma Press, 1944.

Amsden, Charles A. *Navajo Weaving, Its Technique and History.* Albuquerque, N.M.: University of New Mexico Press, 1964.

Athearn, Robert G. *William Tecumseh Sherman and the Settlement of the West.* Norman, Okla.: University of Oklahoma Press, 1956.

Bailey, L. R. *The Long Walk.* Los Angeles: Westernlore Press, 1964.

Burdett, Charles. *The Life of Kit Carson.* Philadelphia: J. Potter & Co., 1869.

Carter, Harvey L. *Dear Old Kit.* Norman, Okla.: University of Oklahoma Press, 1971.

Clarke, Dwight L. *William Tecumseh Sherman: Gold Rush Banker.* San Francisco: San Francisco Historical Society, 1969.

Collier, John. *Indians of the Americas.* New York: New American Library, 1952.

Dale, Edward Everett. *The Indians of the Southwest, A Century of Development under the United States.*

Norman, Okla.: University of Oklahoma Press, 1949; 1971.

Downey, Fairfax. *Indian Wars of the U.S. Army.* New York: Doubleday & Co., 1964.

Dunn, J. P., Jr. *Massacres of the Mountains; A History of the Indian Wars of the Far West, 1815–1875.* New York: Archer House, 1958.

Gilpin, Laura. *The Enduring Navajo.* Austin, Tex.: University of Texas Press, 1968.

Hicks, John D.; Mowery, George E.; and Burke, Robert E. *The Federal Union, A History of the United States to 1877.* Boston: Houghton Mifflin Co., 1964.

Hungerford, Edward. *From Covered Wagon to Streamliner.* New York: Greystone Press, 1941.

Inman, Colonel Henry. *The Old Santa Fe Trail.* New York: The Macmillan Co., 1897.

Lewis, Lloyd. *The Fighting Prophet.* New York: Harcourt, Brace & Co., 1958.

Liddell Hart, Basil Henry. *Sherman, Soldier, Realist, American.* New York: Frederick A. Praeger, Publishers, 1958.

Link, Martin, ed. *Navajo. A Century of Progress, 1868–1968.* Window Rock, Ariz.: The Navajo Tribe, 1968.

Merrill, James M. *William Tecumseh Sherman.* New York: Rand McNally Co., 1971.

O'Connor, Thomas. *The Heritage of the American People.* Boston: Allyn and Bacon, Inc., 1965.

O'Dell, Scott. *Sing down the Moon.* Boston: Houghton Mifflin Co., 1970. (Fiction.)

Potrer, Clyde and Mae, and Sunder, John E. *Matt Field on the Santa Fe Trail.* Norman, Okla.: University of Oklahoma Press, 1960.

Robinson, Doorthy F. *Arizona.* Tempe, Ariz.: Arizona University Press, 1959.

Roland, Albert. *Great Indian Chiefs*. New York: The Macmillan Co., 1966.

Sabin, Henry. *Kit Carson Days*. Chicago: A. C. McClurg & Co., 1944.

Spicer, Edward H. *Cycles of Conquest, the Impact of Spain, Mexico, and the United States on the Indians of the Southwest*. Tempe, Ariz.: University of Arizona Press, 1962.

Stephen, Alexander M. "The Navajo." *The American Anthropologist*. Vol. VI, No. 4 (1893). Washington, D.C.

Tebbel, John. *The Compact History of the Indian Wars*. New York: Hawthorn Books, Inc., 1966.

Underhill, Ruth. *Here Come the Navajo!* Haskell Indian Junior College. Lawrence, Kansas, 1953.

Underhill, Ruth. *The Navajos*. Norman, Okla.: University of Oklahoma Press, 1956, 1971.

Index

Adair, John 131
Ahkeah, Sam 132
Apache Indians 11, 12, 13
Archulets, Chief 30
Ares, Juan 44
Arny, Agent 110, 112
  illustration 94
Arts and Crafts Guild 131,
  133
Arviso, Juan: see Soos
Aubrey, Captain 24
Barboncito 52, 59, 81, 90–91,
  104–105
  illustration 53
Becknell, William 19
Bent, Charles 25
Bosque Redondo Valley 56–57
Brooks, T. L. 47–48
Bureau of Indian Affairs 21,
  29
Corn 6
Calhoun, James S. 29, 31, 32,
  33, 35
Canyon Bonito 35
Canyon de Chelly 14, 35
  illustration 34
Caravans 19
Carleton, James 56–59, 62,
  67, 78, 83, 84

Carson, Christopher 51, 54–
  55, 62–75, 84–86
  illustration 65
Central Pacific Company 48
Central Railroad 112
  see also Santa Fe Railroad
Chaves, Manuel 32
Clark, Major 24
Collier, John 130
Comanche Indians 82, 91
Coronado, Francisco Vasquez
  de 8, 10
Delgadito 81
Dibentsaa 2
Diné 2, 99
Dodd, Agent 89, 100–101,
  104
Dodge, Henry Linn 41–43, 44
Dodge, Henry Chee 126, 132
Doniphan, Colonel 24–26
Dook'o'oslid 2
Education: see Schools
Family life 7
Fort Defiance 36–40, 58, 100,
  107: illus. 38, 39
  illustrations 38, 39
Fort Sumner
  illustration 80
Fort Wingate 63

Franciscans 14–15
Frémont, John C. 26
Gallup, New Mexico 117, 118
Ganado Mucho 52, 67, 105, 107, 113, 118
Garland, General 41
Gilpin, Major 26
Grant, Ulysses 86–87, 105, 111
Guadalupe-Hidalgo, Treaty of 28
Harney, William S. 88
Harrington, John 131
Harvey House 119–120
Hatalhli, Ned 137
Health care 134
    see also Medicine men
Hogans 3, 6
Homestead Act 56
Hopi Indians 13
Hubbel, Don Lorenzo 118, 119
Hunting 7, 8
Indian Peace Commission 88, 90
Indian Rights Association 122
Jamez Pueblos 12, 13
Jasin 40
Keam, Thomas 109–111
Kearney, Stephen 23–26
Kennedy, Robert 137
La Farge, Oliver 131
Lane, William C. 40–41
Largo 27, 30, 42
Lees, John D. 111
Louisiana Purchase 17
Mac Donald, Peter 137
Manuelito 48, 52, 81, 105, 109, 113, 118, 122
    illustration 60
Mascalero Apaches 61
Medicine men 3, 134
Meriwether, David 41

Mexico 17–23
Miller, Agent 109
Mormons 99, 110
Morse, Samuel F. B. 22
Mount Blanca 2
Mount Hesperus 2
Mount Taylor 2, 3
Munroe, John 31, 33
Narbona, Chief 30
Navajo Community College 136–137
Navajo language 131
New Mexico Territory 18, 33, 108
    general Sherman 87
Newby, E. W. 29
Oñate, Juan de 10
Overland Mail Services 46
Pfeiffer, Captain 70, 73
Plummer, Agent 121
Police Force 109, 113–114, 131
Polk, James K. 22
Pony Express 54
Pottery 103
Pueblo Indians 6, 7, 11, 13, 101
Railroads 48–49, 105, 112–113, 115, 117–120
Rainhorse, Ambrose 131
Reorganization Act 130
San Felipe Pueblos 12
San Francisco Mountains 2
Sand painting 3, 103
Sandoval, Antonio 30, 40
Sani, Atsidi 110, 115
Santa Fe, New Mexico 12, 18
Santa Fe Railroad 119
Santa Fe Trail 19
Schools 110, 114, 119, 121, 125, 135
    college 136

Sherman, John 45
Sherman, William T. 45, 46, 55, 85–86, 88, 90–98
  illustration 47
Silversmithing 123
  jewelry 115
Sisnajani 2
Slidell, John 22
Smallpox 85
Soil conservation 127, 129
Soos (Juan Arviso) 81, 104
Spanish exploration 9–17
Stockton, Robert F. 26
Sumner, Colonel 33, 35, 37
  as major 24
Taos, New Mexico 21
Tappan, S. F. 90
Telegraph 50, 55
Terry, Alfred H. 88
Thomas, Lorenzo 78
Trading posts 107, 111

Treaty of Guadalupe-Hidalgo 28
Tso Dzil 2, 3
Tulapai 109
Turquoise 3, 120
Union Pacific Company 48, 49
Ute Indians 44, 46, 63, 66, 69
Vargas, General de 13
Walker, H. T. 28
Wallen, Henry 79
Washington, John M. 29–31
Weaving 6, 108
  illustrations 128; frontespiece
Window Rock, New Mexico 130
Winslow, Arizona 119
World War II
  Navajo language 131
Zeh, William H. 127